Latte Quilt

Bernina
Australia would like to
thank the following people for
their contribution to the Bernina
Latte Quilt project.

Anne Dorahy, Alvena Hall
Joy Harvey, Thea Horsman
Debbie l'Anson, Narelle Morris
Kathy Mackenzie, Kerrie McKeon
Ann Gordon, Sandra Edwards
Sue Box, Wendy Fenwick
Leanne Gardiner

Thanks also to Jack and Maree
Mulvaney for the use of
their home for
photography.

First published in 2001, reprinted 2002 (twice) by Quilters' Resource Inc.
P.O. Box 148850 Chicago IL 60614, Phone 773 278-5695
Text, machine embroidery and project designs copyright © Bernina Australia 2001

Designer: Suzy King
Photography: Simon Blackall, Technical and digital photography: Andrew Payne, Photographix
Produced by the Watermark Press, Sydney
Printed and bound in China

National Library of Congress
Cataloguing-in-Publication Data

Hay, Kerrie.
Latte quilt
ISBN 1 - 889682 - 19 - 5

Latte Quilt

Quilters' Resource publications

ODETTE UELTSCHI-GEGAUF, HER FATHER FRITZ GEGAUF AND HER SON, HANSPETER UELTSCHI—THREE GENERATIONS OF BERNINA'S FOUNDING FAMILY AT STECKBORN, SWITERLAND. HANSPETER NOW HEADS THE COMPANY AFTER THE DEATH OF ODETTE IN 1992.

Foreword

It has always been my belief that although sewing technology has changed significantly over recent years, the sewer always has the desire to be creative. We love to make something with our own hands and this will never change.

At Bernina Australia we recognized this and came up with the idea of the Bernina *Latte Quilt*, which is designed to inspire and rekindle the love of sewing using the sewing machine. It also demonstrates our understanding of the sewer's need to be creative.

The Bernina *Latte Quilt* represents many long hours of embroidery and quilting as the team at Bernina Australia, led by Kerrie Hay, worked towards a common goal. It was exciting to witness the progress of the quilt and the finished product showcases the many possibilities of using the built-in embroidery stitches on your machine along with embroidery motifs, freehand quilting and computer generated and edited designs.

This book guides everyone from the novice to the expert, step-by-step, through the wonders of modern day technology combined with age-old traditions, to produce a truly amazing quilt. It can be simply done using the quilt-as-you-go technique or the more accomplished quilter may choose to embroider the quilt top then quilt the whole quilt—either way the joy of creative accomplishment is the same and is open to all levels of skill.

At Bernina, it is our sincere aim to generate and perpetuate the love of sewing. Use the Bernina *Latte Quilt* to illustrate to the next generation your ability to tap the creative possibilities of the new millennium sewing machines. Share the thrill of turning your dreams into reality by harnessing the power of tomorrow's sewing technology to set your imagination free, leaving a lasting example of your creativity by making the Bernina *Latte Quilt*.

KEVIN ANDERSON
Managing Director
Bernina Australia

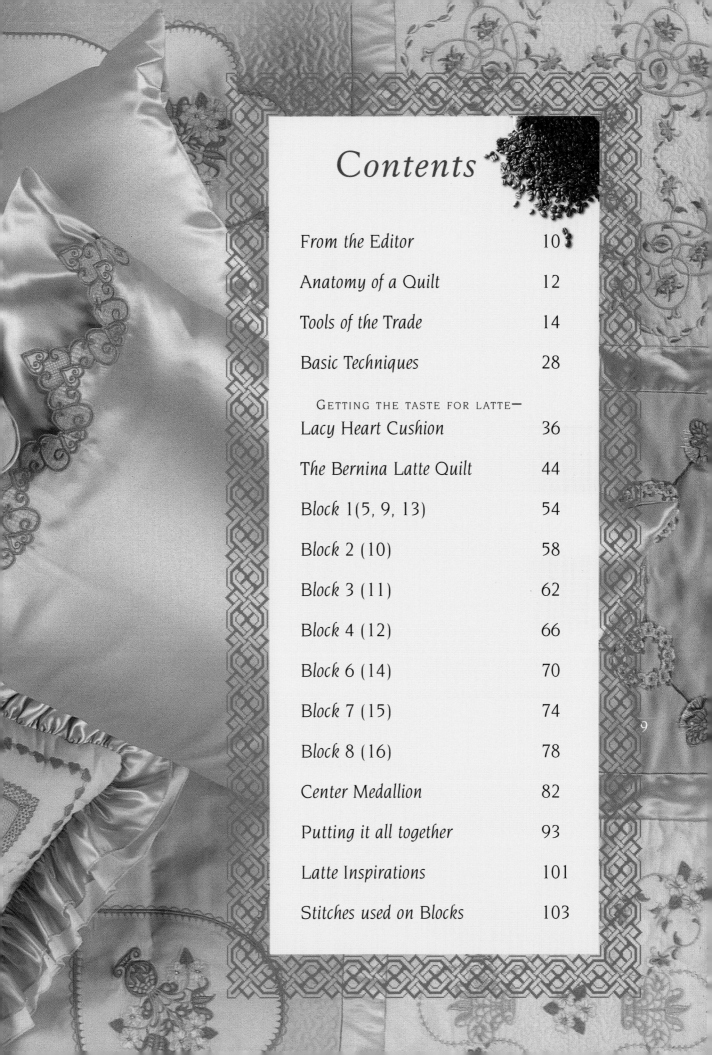

Contents

From the Editor   10

Anatomy of a Quilt   12

Tools of the Trade   14

Basic Techniques   28

GETTING THE TASTE FOR LATTE—

Lacy Heart Cushion   36

The Bernina Latte Quilt   44

Block 1(5, 9, 13)   54

Block 2 (10)   58

Block 3 (11)   62

Block 4 (12)   66

Block 6 (14)   70

Block 7 (15)   74

Block 8 (16)   78

Center Medallion   82

Putting it all together   93

Latte Inspirations   101

Stitches used on Blocks   103

From the Editor

It was not so long ago that the sewing machine was a necessity in every home; a valued appliance for making new garments, linen and furnishings as well as for mending. The hand-operated or treadle sewing machine of the past was a cherished possession; an essential for setting up the family home. And although laws of the late 19th and early 20th centuries prevented a woman inheriting land, even if she had slaved to make it productive, she could lay claim to her mother's sewing machine.

In the 21st century the laws of inheritance are much more equitable and sewing machines have moved with the times as well. Today they have become wonders of computerized technology and creative tools in the hands of their owners as well as the practical and worthy appliances they always were. It is this creative aspect of being able to replicate needlework, embellishment, brocade, lacework, decoration and intricate stitching at the press of a button that sets the modern sewing machine apart from its predecessors.

Thanks also to technology, much of the drudgery of household chores that previously consumed the lion's share of the average woman's time has been reduced and sometimes completely eliminated. But any free time gained as a result of labor-saving devices has been quickly distributed elsewhere by the demands of career, family and community service. Long-term needlework projects are rarely started these days because we live in a world of instant gratification, however we love the stress-relieving, creatively rewarding satisfaction of making something beautiful with our hands, and voilà—the Bernina *Latte* Quilt.

This wonderful project was specifically devised to meet the needs of anyone who wants to be creative with a sewing machine using machine embroidery, stitching and quilting techniques in the Bernina sewing machines. This project has all the hallmarks of a heritage piece—a work of great beauty which will serve as a lesson in loveliness for generations to come.

Sit back, relax with a latte and biscotti and explore the creative possibilities of the Bernina *Latte* Quilt as we guide you step-by-step through each technique so you can create your quilt and experience the pleasure of saying 'I made the Bernina *Latte*.'

KERRIE HAY
National Sewing Promoter
for Bernina in Australia
and New Zealand

10

Anatomy of a Quilt

Understanding the vocabulary used in machine embroidery and quilting
is fundamental when using these techniques and making the Bernina Latte Quilt.
The following most commonly used terms may assist you:

- ACID-FREE MATERIALS—paper products and bonding products (including tissue paper, storage boxes and bonding agents) which do not contain the chemicals normally found in wood and paper which can weaken and destroy fabric over time.

- APPLIQUÉ—a cut-out fabric shape stitched to another piece of fabric.

- BACKING—fabric used for the bottom layer of a quilt.

- **Batting**—the middle layer of a quilt, which provides the loft and warmth.

- **Bias**—the diagonal of a piece of fabric. True bias is at a 45° angle to the lengthwise and crosswise grain of the fabric.

- **Binding**—a strip of fabric used to enclose the edges of a quilt.

- **Block**—a square unit constructed of pieces of fabric which are sewn or embroidered together to form a design. Blocks are joined together to make a quilt top.

- **Borders**—strips of fabric that form the outside edge of the quilt, or surround the center medallion of the quilt to frame the center medallion and the quilt.

- **Free-motion quilting**—involves guiding the fabric through the sewing machine using your hands rather than the pressure from the presser foot and feed dogs.

- **Loft**—the thickness and 'springiness' of the batting or middle layer of a quilt.

- **Machine-guided quilting**—guiding the fabric through the sewing machine using the pressure from the feed dogs (feed dogs up) and the pressure from the presser foot.

- **Medallion quilt** (this term describes the Bernina *Latte Quilt*)—a quilt top with a central motif, usually framed by multiple borders.

- **Miter**—to join corners at a 45° angle.

- **Motif Embroidery**—motifs from embroidery CDs or cards which are embroidered using a hoop that fits onto a domestic sewing machine designed for multi-directional embroidery.

- **Outline quilting**—using a freehand straight stitch through all layers of the quilt to stitch around the outside edge of a design, either appliqué or embroidery, to define the design.

- **Piecing**—stitching together pieces of fabric to create a larger unit.

- **Pre-programmed built-in embroidery stitches**—stitches that are part of the machine's program and come with the sewing machine.

- **Quilt-as-you-go**—quilting each section of the quilt through the batting (but _not_ the backing) then piecing the quilt and stitching-in-the-ditch to secure the three layers of the quilt together. Wonderful way for beginners to start quilting as it eliminates having to cope with the bulk of the quilt when quilting.

- **Quilting**—stitching through three layers of a quilt—the quilt top, batting middle layer and quilt backing—which is designed to hold the fabric layers together and add texture to the quilt.

- **Sashing**—strips of fabric, plain or pieced, which divide the blocks in a quilt.

- **Stipple quilting**—freehand quilting technique of uniform stitching through all layers of the quilt in a continuous meandering line that has no angles and never crosses (intersects) itself.

- **Stitch-in-the-ditch technique**—quilting in a seam line through all three layers of the quilt (top, batting and backing), so the stitching cannot be detected from the quilt front.

Tools of the Trade

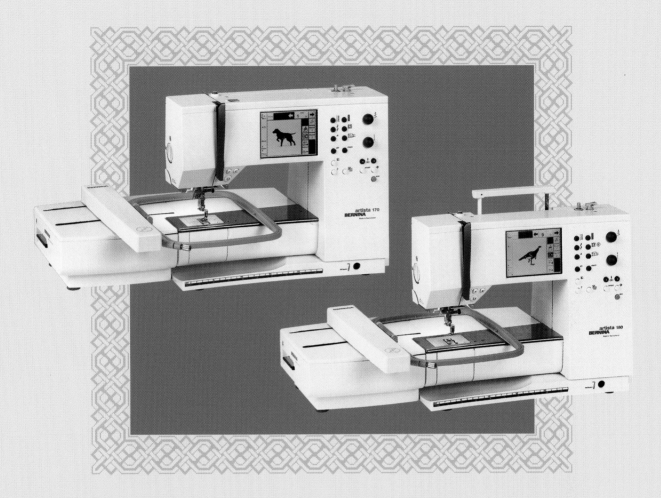

It is essential to have a quality sewing machine such as the Bernina 170/180 before starting on a long-term project. If you are looking for a new sewing machine then shop around and choose carefully, buying from a dealer who offers support services such as on-going technical advice and informative sewing classes to ensure you get the most out of your Bernina sewing machine.

Such basic time-saving features such as bobbin monitor and upper thread sensors which indicate broken threads or that the bobbin is about to run out, needle up/down, clip on feet, knee lift, automatic needle threader, and manual tension over-ride are all included in Bernina sewing machines.

Like all technical equipment, the sewing machine requires proper care to ensure optimum performance.

Ensure your sewing machine is in peak condition by following a few basic guidelines:

—Always have your machine serviced regularly by an authorized technician

—Clean your machine regularly ensuring it is lint free in both the

bobbin area and the upper thread path; such products as 'Dust-a-Way' canned air are very handy for doing this

—Oil your machine regularly according to the manufacturers instructions

—Change your needle often; a bent or blunt needle affects the quality of your sewing. Also, choose the appropriate needle to suit the technique and fabric type. •

TIP: When changing thread during embroidery, clip the thread close to the thread reel then pull the thread through the tension disk in the direction it would normally pass. This ensures any lint or shredded thread is caught in the tension disks. The same applies to the bobbin: clip the thread close to the bobbin then pull the thread through the tension when changing a bobbin.

Bernina Designer Software
Embroidery Software frees the Creative Spirit

The **Artista v3.0** software provides a range of options for creating custom embroidery designs. Sewers can choose one of four software packages appropriate to a range of needs and skill levels.

—**Artista Editor** allows the user to customize and edit designs, including reshaping objects, changing colors choosing from 40 alphabets and reading/writing to Magic Box (a device that, when used with a personal computer, allows the user to translate embroidery designs from one embroidery card type [format] to another.) Cross stitch is available as an optional extra.

—**Artista Auto Designer** includes all Artista Editor features and adds auto digitizing and a link to third-party image-processing programs; Photosnap and Cross Stitch are also available as an option, allowing users to digitize their own personal photos and turn them into fine embroidery.

—**Artista Designer** includes all the features above plus additional appliqué, font, pattern, fancy fill and Photosnap and Cross stitch options.

—**Artista Super/Designer** software includes all the above features plus Photosnap and Cross Stitch software.

Bernina offers Artista Cross Stitch and Photosnap software as an option for *certain* Artista embroidery software products. The Artista Cross Stitch software gives users the power to replicate traditional hand stitched designs and lettering from clip art, cross stitch charts or freehand, and to combine cross-stitch designs with Artista's digitizing and editing features.

Photosnap is user-friendly software, which gives the user the possibility to convert a portrait (photo in BMP format) into a uni-colored embroidery motif.

Version 1, 2, & 3 Software

The numbered version of the Bernina Designer software indicates the order in which it was released with each new version adding to the capabilities of the previous one. The Bernina Designer Software is very sophisticated software designed to interface with a domestic sewing machine with the capabilities of commercial software allowing the end user to scan in designs then automatically digitize (determines the placement of stitching within the pattern). The result can then be downloaded to the sewing machine or to a memory card to be stitched out by a domestic sewing machine. Each version however will allow you to utilize the functions necessary to access the techniques needed for the *Bernina Latte Quilt*. Although the software is very user friendly, a working knowledge of computers and Windows® is recommended for frustration-free results.

Artlink Software

This software provides many editing features to personalize .**ART** embroidery designs. Some of the editing features allow one to: rotate, mirror, and re-size designs, change colors, show design in artistic view and multiple undo/redo functions. Independent of all this, Artlink is programmed with 24 built-in embroidery designs.

CPS *version 3 and 4*

These versions of the CPS software are available for the Bernina 170, 170QPE and 180. This software provides 350 stitches to choose from and download to your Artista machine. In addition this software allows one to choose from 250 embroidery designs to download to the embroidery module. The embroidery designs and stitches can also be changed as often as needed or desired.

Bernina Large and Medium Hoops

The large hoop comes as standard equipment with the Bernina embroidery module. The medium hoop is an optional extra. Choose a hoop that best fits the design to be embroidered on your machine. Large hoop is 200mm x 155mm and the medium hoop is 130mm x 100mm.

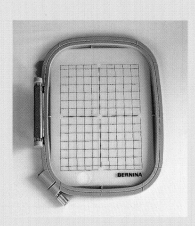 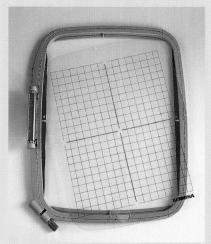

Transparent Grid Templates

These grid templates come with each hoop size, with the embroidery surface marked in 1cm squares. The center and the corners of these are marked with holes for transferring markings to fabric. When the block fabric (with the dividing lines and the center position of the motif to be embroidered marked) is placed on the self-adhesive tear-away in the hoop directly under the needle, place the template in the inner hoop over the fabric so the word BERNINA is at the front (by the arrows) and can be read.

Doing the above and aligning marked positioning lines on the fabric with lines on the grid will ensure that the fabric is over the self-adhesive stabilizer in the hoop straight (both vertically and horizontally) to ensure the design is stitched straight and in the correct position. Should the marked position on the fabric be a little off center then use the arrows to move the design slightly— either up, down or to either side.

Remove the template using the finger hole in the template then embroider the design.

Machine Feet:

STANDARD FOOT NO 1

The standard foot (comes with all Bernina sewing machines) is used for basic sewing with straight and reverse stitches that do not require dense satin stitching. This foot has a slight indentation at the front and rear of the needle which allows the foot to move easily in both directions on the fabric.

ZIPPER FOOT NO 4

The Zipper foot (comes with all Bernina sewing machines) is used for inserting zippers and is designed to allow the sewer to stitch close to the zipper coils while feeding both the fabric and the zipper evenly though the machine.

DARNING FOOT NO 9

The Darning/Embroidery Foot is designed for a variety of freehand techniques, especially computerized machine embroidery done automatically in a hoop. Freehand techniques require that the feed dogs be in the down position, allowing the sewer to guide the movement of the fabric (in place of the feed dogs) in the direction of her/his choice. This foot does not come in contact with the feed dogs, rather, as the sewer moves the fabric along the desired path, the vertical spring action of the foot holds the fabric down as the needle pulls away, eliminating flagging or lifting.

TIP: *All freehand techniques require practice. It is advisable to experiment with these techniques before working on a project.*

It is recommended that:

—the sewer sits directly in front of the machine so she/he can see the machine needle clearly

—the hands rest on the fabric on either side of the foot/needle to place pressure on the fabric as well as guiding it

—stitches are kept even by following the rule 'fast machine and slow hands'. This means running the machine at a moderate to fast but even speed while guiding the hands/fabric with an even, smooth movement.

If stitches are too small, either reduce the machine speed, or alternately move the hands faster. If stitches are too large or erratic, increase the motor speed or guide the fabric a little slower.

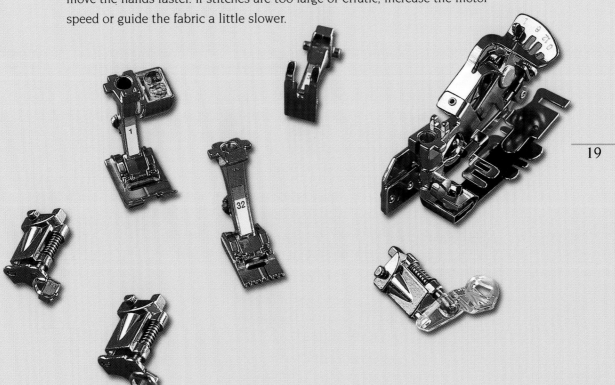

19

OPEN TOE EMBROIDERY FOOT NO 20

The Open-toe Embroidery Foot, either 5mm or 9mm, is designed to be used with compact or satin stitches, the wedge-shaped indentation on the underside of the foot allows dense or bulky stitches to glide easily under it thus eliminating stitch build-up which would inhibit the smooth feeding-thru of the fabric. The open area between the toes of the foot allows the sewer a clear view of the needle and stitching area—this is especially useful in stitch building and in appliqué techniques that require stitching around straight-sided, curved or composite shapes.

FREEHAND QUILTING FOOT NO 29

The Freehand Quilting Foot can be used for a wide range of free-motion techniques requiring the feed dogs to be lowered, such as freehand outline, echo and stipple quilting. This foot is specifically designed for quilting with high loft battings allowing the quilter the freedom to use any technique that is desired.

PINTUCK FOOT NO 32

The Pintucking Feet have equidistant parallel grooves on the underside of each foot and are from a family of feet that comes in many sizes. Their primary use is for sewing pintucks on fine to lightweight fabrics, in conjunction with a twin needle but can also be used for stitching techniques that benefit from having parallel grooves on the underside of the foot. Pintucks can be shaped, corded and shaded.

The number 32 foot has seven 1.3 mm grooves on the underside of the foot for perfectly spaced pintucks. When sewing pintucks, always start with the center groove for the first pintuck, then for parallel pintucks place the first pintuck in one of the side grooves. The quilting guide can also be used for parallel pintucks to keep them evenly placed when the desired gap is wider than the foot.

PATCHWORK ¼ INCH FOOT NO 37

The Patchwork Foot offers a guide for stitching ¼in seams, typically used for traditional patchwork. The side edges of the foot are exactly ¼in from the center needle position. The inner edges of the front of the toes on the foot are ⅛in from the center needle position, which is an asset when stitching miniature quilts. The under side of the foot is very flat with a narrow groove for the stitching to pass through, thus providing more support for the fabric. The foot also has ¼in notches at the front and the back of the foot, equal distance from the needle to assist in turning corners when a ¼in seam is required.

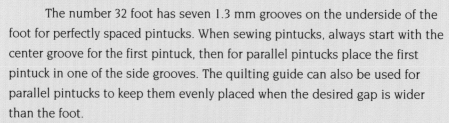

WALKING FOOT

(Check with your dealer as to which foot number you need to suit your machine.)

The Walking Foot or even-feed foot is designed to feed fabrics that don't usually feed easily or evenly through the machine, such as pile fabrics like velvets or corduroy; slippery fabrics such as satin and silks; sticky fabrics like leather and vinyl; and layered fabrics such as quilts. This foot is also useful when matching stripes, prints or checked fabrics eliminating the need to pin. In quilts where the fabric layers need to be held together with the 'stitch-in-the-ditch' technique (sewing down the groove in the seam line holding the quilt top, batting and backing together) the walking foot feeds the layers evenly eliminating puckering. This foot comes with two types of feet: one for normal sewing and an open-toe which gives a clear view of the stitch line.

THE RUFFLER FOOT NO 86

The Ruffler Foot is a time saving device that is used when ruffling is required, such as with frills or skirting that needs to be pleated and is ideal for garments and home decorating projects.

The ruffler can be adjusted to set the pleating frequency, for example a pleat with every stitch, every six stitches, or every twelfth stitch. It can also be set so no pleats are sewn. The depth of the pleat can also be adjusted depending on how full the desired frill should be.

Needles

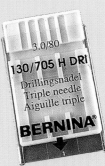

Needles can determine stitch quality and are therefore one of the most important tools when sewing a project. Needles are designed to meet the needs of the stitch and fabric type such as jeans needles, embroidery needles, and leather needles.

NEEDLES USED IN THIS BOOK ARE:

—size-90 embroidery needles which have a sharp point to easily penetrate the fabric and have a larger eye so the thread does not shred when sewing embroidery stitches

—size-80 jeans needle can also be used for machine embroidery or quilt piecing

—twin needle 1.8mm or 2mm twin needle for corded pintucks or twin needle quilting or stitching. It is important to make sure that the needles are always changed otherwise thread pulls in the fabric will result

—second spool holder for the above

—triple needle which, as the name implies, is made up of three evenly spaced needles. You will need to have a third spool holder when using these needles for the third reel of thread

—multi-spool holder for the above

—size-80 quilting needles used for freehand quilting

—hand beading needle for sewing on the beads

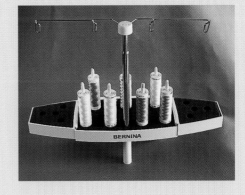

21

Thread

Most types of thread can be used in machine embroidery and quilting but always look for quality being mindful of color consistency, strength, luster and durability.

Threads are gauged by denier or thickness—80-denier being the finest and 30-denier being the heaviest.

The Bernina *Latte Quilt* uses a variety of threads depending on the technique being used.

    Mettler Poly Sheen (Mettler Silky Sheen) 40-denier, Fawn No 934, (670) Oat No 761 (761) and Eggshell No 101 (853) are used for embroidery, fancy built-in stitches and twin needling. They produce a sheen on the finished embroidery.

    Mettler polyester cream thread for quilting and construction.

    Mettler bobbin fill or pre-wound bobbins are used in the bobbin case for all embroidery. You may also choose to use a Mettler polyester thread on the metal bobbins, but as the thread is thicker the bobbins do not go as far as the pre-wound ones which use a much finer thread.

    Monofilament thread is a transparent thread used for 'stitching-in-the-ditch' in the seams between blocks and sashing.

    Mettler Cordonnet thread in white is used to cord the pintucks.

    Beading thread has extra strength and durability and is used to hand bead.

Stabilizers

All fabric that is to be embroidered needs to be stabilized in order to add stability to the fabric so it does not pucker or pull-in during embroidering or after the embroidery is complete. There is a wide range of stabilizers on the market today designed to accommodate specific sewing requirements including:

    Stick-It-All or self-adhesive tear-away is a standard medium tack (degree of adherence) sticky-backed tear-away stabilizer made of 100% washable and dry cleanable polyester that looks and tears like paper. It comes with a protective covering which is removed once the stabilizer has been placed in the hoop. Cut a piece to fit your hoop, hoop it with the paper backing side up then score around the inside edge of the hoop with a pin and remove the protective paper leaving the sticky surface uppermost in the hoop—this is the surface to which the fabric is directly applied for embroidery. When embroidery is complete the fabric is removed from the stabilizer, the resulting hole patched from the back so the stabilizer can be re-used many times and is consequently very economical.

It can also be used when embroidering small fabric areas on ready-made

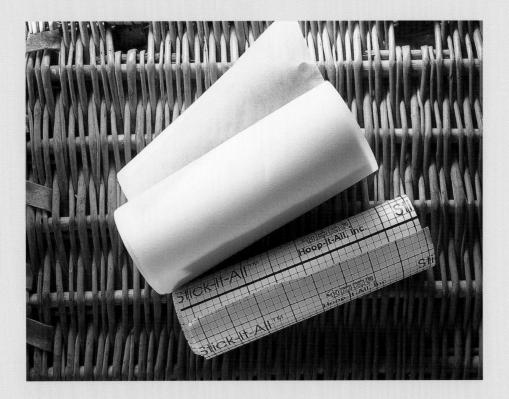

items such as baby socks, ribbons, ties, collars, cuffs and any garments. Self-adhesive tear-away also eliminates hoop marks on fabrics such as velvet and satin, preventing damage and shifting of fine fabrics during embroidery and prevents stretching or puckering of fabric due to embroidery.

Self-adhesive tear-away ensures perfect placement eliminating the need to re-hoop fabric. Instead, by placing the fabric under the needle in the exact position required ensures perfect embroidery placement results every time.

Should a build-up of sticky residue be found on the needle after a lengthy period of sewing, wipe the needle clean with a tissue or small piece of fabric that is dipped in methylated spirits or a suitable solvent.

🔖 Stitch-n-tear stabilizer is placed at the back of fabric that is embroidered with built-in decorative stitching to prevent distortion to the fabric or stitching. It can also be used at the back of fabric that has batting attached to it ensuring perfec stitching and preventing the batting attaching to the teeth of the feed dogs thus retarding perfect feeding of fabric and stitch. The stitch-n-tear is then carefully removed from the back of the fabric so as not to damage the stitching.

General Sewing Requirements

There are many products available which support, improve and add to the professional finish of machine embroidery and quilting projects. Readily available, they are a must for the 21st century sewer.

🔖 *Rotary cutter*—a tool with a round blade used to cut straight lines through single and multiply layers of fabric with speed and accuracy.

🔖 *Olfa mat*—a self-healing mat designed to be used under a rotary cutter.

🔖 *Quilting ruler and 15in square*—a plastic measure divided into imperial measurements and used in conjunction with a rotary cutter and self-healing cutting mat to ensure straight accurate lines.

🔖 *Vliesofix/Wonderunder*—double-sided fusible web which comes on a backing paper. Bonding is activated by steam and heat. Perfect for accurately attaching one piece of fabric to another as in appliqué.

🔖 *Fusible batting*—Freudenbergs H640 is a batting that has one side treated with a heat and steam dissolving bond that allows the batting to be fused to the back of fabric that is to be quilted—ideal for quilt-as-you-go technique.

🔖 *Appliqué mat*—used during heat-bonding to protect the fabric and the iron and to absorb glue substances from bonding agents.

🔖 *Fabric marking pens*—either air or water fading fabric-marking pens ensure guide lines will not be evident on the finished project.

🔖 *Quilting pins*—fine, extra long pins with glass heads preferably.

🔖 *Quilters safety pins*—used to hold the fabric layers of a quilt together to ensure smooth quilting when sewing.

🔖 *Dress making shears*—for cutting large fabric pieces.

🔖 *Small sharp scissors*—for cutting out appliqué fabric shapes.

🔖 *Small clips*—for cutting threads.

🔖 *Paper scissors.*

🔖 *Quality steam iron*—an industrial strength vertical steam iron is preferable

Basic Equipment

- Bernina 170/180

- Bernina Designer Software Version 1, 2 or 3 or Bernina Artlink software

- Bernina CPS software for personal stitch choice

- Bernina *Latte Quilt* design CD that accompanies this book

- Artistic Design multi formatted CDs: Beautiful borders, Artistic Adornments and Lace and Romantic designs for additional designs that go with the *Latte Quilt* designs (optional)

- Studio Bernina Beautiful borders Card No 527 and Lace and Romantic Designs Card No 126, also for additional designs (optional)

- Bernina machine feet

- Bernina machine needles

- Fabric

- Batting

- Vliesofix/Wonderunder

- Stitch-n-tear

- Self-adhesive tear-away stabilizer

- Mettler threads

- Monofilament thread

- Pre-wound bobbins

- Quilting ruler and tape measure

- Rotary cutter, self-healing cutting mat and 15in quilters square

- Vellum (112gsm) tracing paper

- Adhesive spray

- Reducing and shading glass

- General sewing requirements

27

Basic Techniques

Decorative work undertaken on a sewing machine is considered to be machine embellishment or embroidery. With careful planning, a vivid imagination and a little practice, you will soon be on your way to creating you own innovative designs.

In this section we have included some of the basic techniques used in the BERNINA LATTE QUILT *to get you started, so read the instructions carefully and practice the techniques you are unsure of first.*

The *Bernina Latte Quilt* is an embroidered, medallion quilt featuring a center medallion surrounded by sashed blocks. After each block is embroidered, fusible batting is ironed to its back and then it is quilted before being joined into rows of sashed blocks.

The above technique is the easiest method of quilting as it reduces the bulk of the fabric that has to pass under the machine. Attaching the completed quilt top to the backing fabric with the stitch-in-the-ditch method of sewing in the groove created by a seam line will quilt the three layers together and does involve the whole quilt. With the major part of the quilting completed, it is an easier procedure than quilting from scratch.

Appliqué

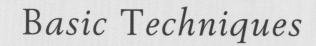

Appliqué is the technique of applying a fabric shape to a larger piece of fabric. The availability of Vliesofix/Wonderunder (double-sided fusible web that bonds to the back of the fabric to be appliquéd, seals the cut-out edges of the fabric and allows it to be heat-bonded to a larger piece of fabric), has simplified this technique.

The double-sided fusible web comes with a paper backing and is ironed to the back of the fabric. From the paper side, the fabric is cut out in the desired shape then applied to another fabric using steam and heat, as the bonding agent in the fusible web is a steam and heat activated.

Remember to leave the backing paper in place when cutting out and only remove it when you are ready to iron the appliqué in place.

The raw fabric edges are usually sealed with a small satin stitch or in this case, with rows of embroidery stitches which not only seal the edges but extend the design as well. Appliqué is a good starting point for beginners.

Applying Vliesofix/Wonderunder

It is important to remember that Vliesofix/Wonderunder is a steam and heat dissolving bond, so use plenty of steam or spray with water before ironing the web to the back of fabric.

If you are tracing a design from a pattern, remember to trace on the rough side of the Vliesofix/Wonderunder (not the paper side) if it is not symmetrical so that when the shape is applied to the back of the fabric it will not mirror the design. Label or number all pieces if you decide to cut out all the appliqué pieces at one time.

Applying Fusible Batting

Fusible batting is a batting that has one side treated with a steam and heat activated bonding agent. The wrong side of the fabric sits over the rough side (bonding side) of the batting and is ironed in place using a hot steam iron from the right side of the fabric.

Done correctly this application is permanent, holding the fabric securely to the batting without any puckers. It also eliminates the need to pre-wash fabrics because when the quilt is washed, the batting holds the fabric in place so it cannot shrink.

Fusible batting is made by Freudenberg and comes in two weights: H630 a lightweight batting and H640 a slightly heavier one.

The batting in the *Latte Quilt* was applied to the blocks once the motif embroidery was completed so it could be quilted and embellished before being joined.

Cutting Techniques

SCISSORS

Ideally you should have three pairs of good scissors, including a large pair of dressmakers shears, a small sharp pointed pair for delicate cutting and those fiddly bits and paper scissors for cutting paper and templates. It is also a good idea to have a pair of snips to cut machine embroidery threads between color changes.

ROTARY CUTTER AND MAT

The rotary cutter and self-healing cutting mat have proved to be a great asset to the quilter allowing the user to cut several layers of fabric at one go without distortion. Use the cutter and mat with a plastic quilting ruler to ensure speed with accuracy.

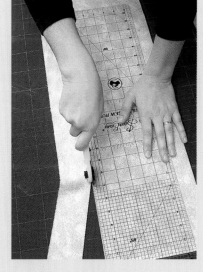

Place the fabric over the marked grid on the self-healing cutting mat aligning the edge to be cut with a line on the mat. Place the ruler over the fabric so it aligns with the cutting grid line on either side of the fabric, lay your left hand (if you are right handed) flat on the ruler so the 'ring' or fourth finger lies flat against the opposite edge of the ruler to the aligned cutting edge and press your hand flat. The ruler will not move when you run the rotary cutter along the

29

alignment edge of the ruler as it pushes against the ring finger which holds it in place. This method also keeps fingers away from the rotary cutter. Always remember to close the rotary cutter after use, as it is very sharp.

Stitching Techniques

Using the correct feet, needles and stabilizers, which are explained in the Tools of the Trade section from page 18, ensures perfect results, so refer to this section before stitching.

BUILT-IN EMBROIDERY STITCHES

Bernina have a vast array of built-in fancy/embroidery stitches which used alone are great, but when combined in 'stitch building' are spectacular. These stitches are used for appliqué and to connect the embroidery motifs, thus creating one design. Any embroidery stitch based on a satin stitch is an ideal base for appliqué as it first seals the raw fabric edges then adds a decorative finish.

An embroidery needle, Mettler 40, embroidery threads, pre-wound bobbin, open-toe embroidery foot 5mm or 9mm, size 80 jeans needle and tear-a-way stabilizer at the back of the fabric, ensure professional stitch quality.

Remember you are working with a state-of-the-art sewing machine so let it do the work. Just keep your fabric straight and let the machine feed it through. Pulling or retarding the fabric feeding will result in stitch distortion.

Bobbin tension should be tight and the upper tension may have to be manually over-ridden to achieve perfect results. Being able to see bobbin thread from the top of your work is very disappointing. Correct tension is essential for achieving perfect results.

TIP: *When using embroidery stitches around curves, it is a good idea to shorten the pattern length. Use your single pattern default and the knee lift to pivot after every pattern is complete.*

TWIN NEEDLE STITCHING

A twin needle is usually used in conjunction with a pintucking foot to create pintucks, either plain or corded. It can also be used with embroidery stitching and two different thread colors (remember to use your twin needle default function to adjust the width of the stitch) as well as parallel rows of stitching/quilting using the same or different thread colors.

Twin needle stitching can also be used to quilt in a grid with either vertical and horizontal lines or diagonal lines. Use the quilting guide to ensure accurate spacing between rows.

Corded pintucks require a cord to be placed up through the hole in the base plate (which is accessed from the underside of the plate with the bobbin door open). This cord then travels under the fabric that is being pintucked under the center of the foot and out the back. The twin needles sew over the fabric and catch the cord up into the pintuck so it is held in place with a zigzag stitch from the underside of the fabric. This technique is used on block No. 7 and No. 15 using the underside of the corded pintuck, sewn in a grid, as the right side of the stitching to achieve an unusual effect.

NOTE: *Twin needle sewing requires two reels of thread. Attach your second spool holder and direct one thread though the left side of the tension disk and the other through the right. Then thread the threads through their corresponding needles.*

TRIPLE NEEDLE STITCHING

This, as the name implies, requires the use of a needle that has three needles in a row, equally spaced. You may need to purchase a multi-spool holder to accommodate the third reel of thread and direct two threads through one side of the tension disk and one on the other side.

Using two or three shades of thread, stitch/quilt in a grid using the quilting guide to give accurate spacing between the rows of stitching to create wondrous effects.

FREEHAND STITCHING

Many different effects can be achieved using this technique such as stipple, continuous design and outline quilting, along with manually-guided embroidery such as thread painting or shading. Freehand requires the feed dogs to be lowered and you use a freehand foot.

As the feed dogs are lowered the sewer controls the fabric. You may find it easier to control the movement of the fabric by placing it in a hoop. Faster machine speed than hand and fabric movement along with regulated fabric movement, ensures even stitching.

Machine Quilting

Quilting stitches are like icing on a cake. They enhance the appearance and make the texture ever so much better!

The following are machine-quilting techniques used in the *Latte Quilt*:

—stitch-as-you-go is quilting, usually a block, sashing and/or borders, before the quilt is pieced. Then stitch-in-the-ditch (freehand or machine guided) to hold the quilted top to the backing

—stitch-in-the-ditch is quilting in the channel formed by a seamline, so the stitching is not seen from the front of the quilt but it is stitched through to the quilt backing and holds the layers of the quilt together: other quilting sewn at the same time can be freehand or machine-guided stitching

—outline quilting is usually sewn with a transparent thread or a fine thread that exactly matches the fabric that the outline is stitched on. It is used to define a motif, fabric or embroidery by quilting around the outline. This can be freehand or machine-guided stitching

—continuous line quilting is done freehand using a fine thread such as an 80-denier and follows a quilting design that is copied onto the fabric to be quilted and is stitched in one continuous line. Using a fine thread makes it easier to stitch over previous stitching, to continue the line without noticing a build up of thread and stitches

—stipple quilting is usually used to fill background areas or to create texture on a quilt. The stitch can be worked in any direction, using a matching, monofil or contrasting fine thread.

Stipple quilting is a continuous meandering line that has no angles and does not intersect itself and it is formed with straight uniform-length stitches. If this type of quilting is a feature on your quilt or in a contrasting thread it is advisable to practice to ensure uniform stitch length and even curves. Stipple quilting must be good to be effective, even brilliant. Poor stipple quilting is a blight on your quilt.

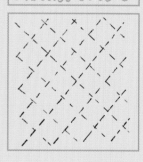

—Grids, either on the straight or diagonal, are achieved using the walking foot, a straight stitch and the quilting guide to ensure the lines are parallel and equally spaced. Quilting using this method is another way to fill in background areas on a quilt or in smaller center areas or borders created by other quilting designs, embroidery or appliqué.

Motif Embroidery

All top end domestic sewing machines such as the Bernina 170/180 have the capacity to interface with a computer—utilizing design software to design, edit, copy, download from the internet and read embroidery CDs then download the designs via an interface cable to the machine to automatically sew the design motif using an embroidery hoop.

These designs motifs can be used separately or together to form another design connected with built-in stitching.

BERNINA CPS SOFTWARE (CUSTOMISED PATTERN SELECTION)
The CPS is used to download stitches and embroidery motifs. The following instructions are for editing design No. 8 from collection No. 5 used in Block No. 4 and No.12. Using the Bernina software, this design is edited, re-colored and resized to suit the block.

You will need the following:
—Bernina Artista 170/180 and Embroidery Module plus accessories
—Bernina CPS software and personal design card
—one of the Bernina Embroidery Software packages: Editor, or Auto Designer or Designer (V1, V2, or V3)

DOWNLOADING A DESIGN FROM CPS TO YOUR ARTISTA
Check that your machine/embroidery unit is connected correctly to the computer and a personal card is in the machine and turn the machine and computer on and open the CPS software.

NOW ACTION THE FOLLOWING COMMANDS:
—click on the **Embroidery Module**
—click on the **Exchange CPS** button on the tool bar
—select design **No. 8** from **Collection No.** 5 then send the design to the machine
—turn the sewing machine off then on to activate the new design
—open **the design** (No 8) **on your machine** and save to **a personal design** card.

TRANSFER THE DESIGN TO THE EMBROIDERY SOFTWARE.
Using your chosen Bernina software, action the following commands:
—**open** the software
—**open File**, select **Card/Machine Read** command from the drop down dialog box
—**select design** No. 8 saved on the personal **design card** and bring it into the software
—**name** and **save design No.** 8 to **My Designs** folder. (Remember to write the name down for ease of use when you need to recall it later.) The colors have changed from the CPS; this will be corrected later in the exercise

Editing the Design

—select **one of the small balls in the center of the design by highlighting it** (magenta) press **delete** then repeat this for all five balls
—**highlight** to select **the right side of the design** (magenta)
—**use the** arrow keys **on the keyboard to move the design while it is still** highlighted **to the left, until both halves of the design are touching in the center at the bottom stems and leaves**
—select **Settings Menu** then select **Thread Colors** from the drop down dialog box to change the colors to the following:

Mettler Poly Sheen-numeric.

Colour 1 - 934 - Fawn
Colour 2 - 761 - Oat
Colour 3 - 934 - Fawn
Colour 4 - 101 - Eggshell

—select **Arrange** menu then select
Auto Center from the drop down dialog box to center the design.
This will enable you to print a template with the cross hairs in the center of the design
—select **Print** and print the design on vellum (112gsm) tracing paper to be used as a template
—select **Save** and name the new design

33

SEND THE DESIGN TO THE ARTISTA

—select **Write to Machine** on the toolbar to send the new design to the machine to be embroidered following the directions for Block No. 4 and No. 12.

Templates

NOTE: *All embroidery motifs are embroidered either on the straight or diagonal lines marked in preparation on each fabric block, making templates easy to use and ensuring accurate placement.*

Templates are necessary for accurate placement of embroidery designs and either come with the embroidery card/CD or can be printed via the design's software through the computer onto Vellum (112gsm) tracing paper which is inexpensive and will easily feed through your printer or photocopy machine. This gives the user a transparent reproduction of the embroidery motif so that accurate placement lines can be marked in the desired position on the fabric to ensure a perfectly placed motif.

These templates are provided with this book with the appropriate center positioning lines (vertical and horizontal) marked as well as the starting position of each design.

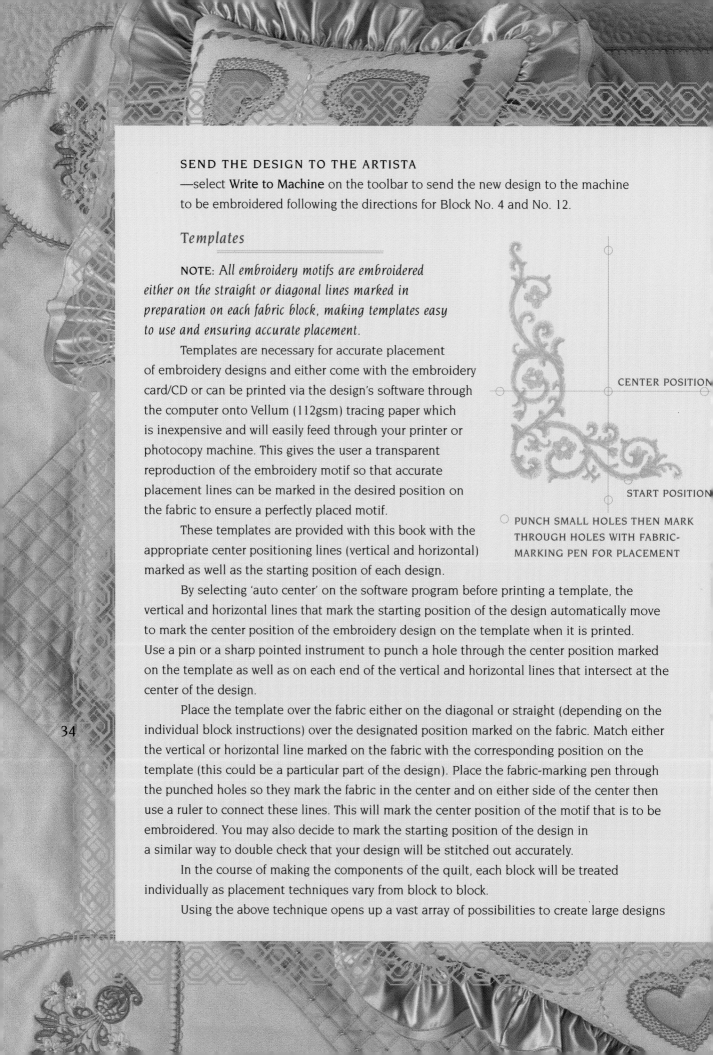

CENTER POSITION

START POSITION

○ PUNCH SMALL HOLES THEN MARK THROUGH HOLES WITH FABRIC-MARKING PEN FOR PLACEMENT

By selecting 'auto center' on the software program before printing a template, the vertical and horizontal lines that mark the starting position of the design automatically move to mark the center position of the embroidery design on the template when it is printed. Use a pin or a sharp pointed instrument to punch a hole through the center position marked on the template as well as on each end of the vertical and horizontal lines that intersect at the center of the design.

Place the template over the fabric either on the diagonal or straight (depending on the individual block instructions) over the designated position marked on the fabric. Match either the vertical or horizontal line marked on the fabric with the corresponding position on the template (this could be a particular part of the design). Place the fabric-marking pen through the punched holes so they mark the fabric in the center and on either side of the center then use a ruler to connect these lines. This will mark the center position of the motif that is to be embroidered. You may also decide to mark the starting position of the design in a similar way to double check that your design will be stitched out accurately.

In the course of making the components of the quilt, each block will be treated individually as placement techniques vary from block to block.

Using the above technique opens up a vast array of possibilities to create large designs

34

made up of several similar, the same or different motifs to form a new design. This technique is used on all the blocks in the *Latte Quilt*.

MAKING TWISTED RIBBON TREE TRUNKS

For the Topiary Hearts blocks, No. 7 and No. 15

1) Measure out approximately 3 yards of 2mm fawn silk ribbon then double it up until it measures 1½ yards, keeping the ends even. Set up the machine in bobbin winding mode, then place one end of the folded silk ribbon through one of the holes in the bobbin and place the bobbin on the winder with the ribbons secured and engage the bobbin winder.

2) Hold the free end of the ribbons out from the sewing machine, so the ribbons are taut, then start the bobbin winding; this will twist the ribbon. When you feel the ribbon is twisted sufficiently take the end of the ribbons in your hand to the bobbin folding the length of twisted ribbon in two, and secure the fold with your other hand. Carefully remove the ribbon from the bobbin, keeping a tight grip on the ribbons in both hands—one hand on either end of the twisted ribbon. When the ribbons are released they will twist back on themselves forming a twisted cord. Knot the free ends securely to ensure the cord remains twisted.

MAKING MONDO GRASS

For the Topiary Hearts blocks, No. 7 and No. 15

1) Use the lead pencil to draw a 2in x 1in rectangle center in the cardboard template then use the paper scissors to cut this out.

2) Use the three threads Oat, Eggshell and Fawn (together) to wrap around the center of the cardboard template lengthwise (over the cut out section, twenty times (or the desired thickness)

CARDBOARD FRAME FOR MONDO GRASS

SEW BETWEEN

4" 2 ¼"

STITCHING 1"

2"

THREADS WRAPPED AROUND APPROX. 20 TIMES

CENTER

CUT OUT SECTION DENOTED BY BROKEN LINES

3) Select a 9mm zigzag stitch with matching thread in the needle and bobbin, the 9mm open-toe foot and the feed-dogs lowered. Stitch forwards and reverse several times over the cords in open section of the cardboard—refer to cardboard frame diagram. It is not necessary to cover the cords as you would for a tassel, this just holds them securely together. Remember to tie off at the beginning and end of the stitching.

4) Cut the threads at both ends of the cardboard template to release the threads.

5) Fold the threads in halves lengthwise through the center of the wrapped section then sew a bar tack over at the end of the wrapped section secured with straight stitching. Remove from the machine and trim ends.

6) Repeat step 2 to 5 another seven times as eight pieces of Mondo grass are needed for the pots.

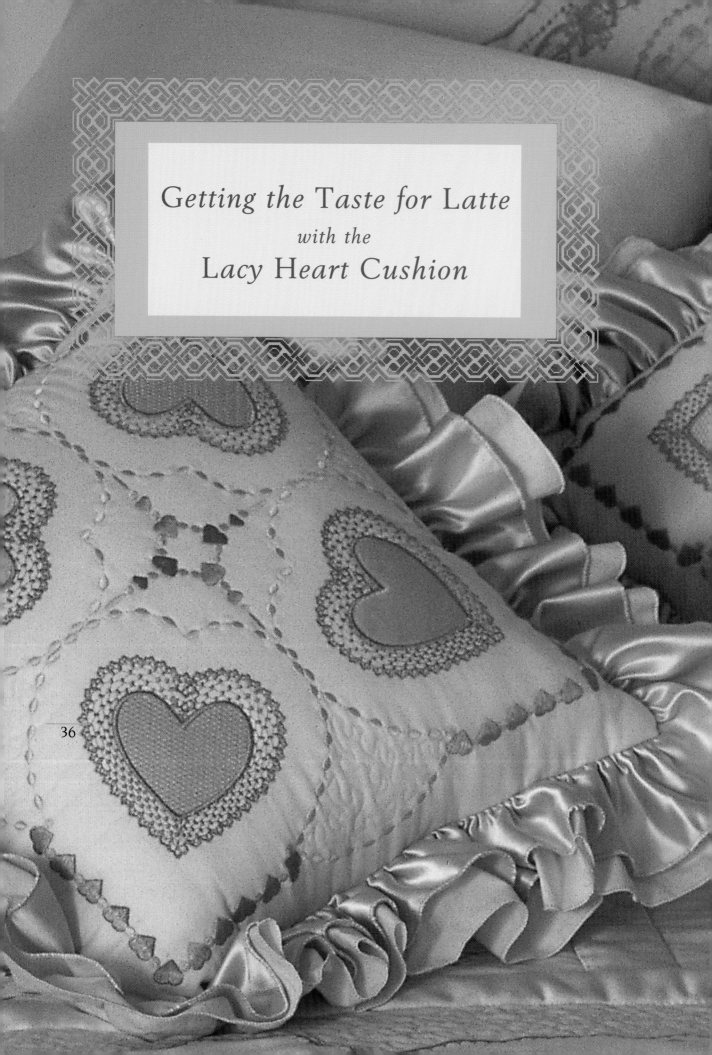

Getting the Taste for Latte
with the
Lacy Heart Cushion

36

These delightful cushions are a wonderful way to try your hand at the techniques used in the Latte Quilt with embroidery from the Lace and Romantic Design CD from Artistic Designs. For a free download of these designs, go to www.berninausa.com. The materials list gives all requirements needed to make one cushion but refer to the Techniques Section on page 28 for specific techniques. This way you will have to read the techniques and practice them before starting on the quilt.

Materials

- Bernina 170/180 embroidery machine
- Bernina software
- Lace and Romantic Design CD from Artistic Designs*
- Bernina Overlocker/Serger set for a three-thread rolled hem
- 26in cream quilters muslin for cushion and frill
- 18in *latte* colored satin for frill and appliqué
- 18in square fusible batting
- 6in strip Vliesofix/Wonderunder
- 18in zip
- *Machine feet*: Standard foot No. 1, 5mm open-toe foot No. 20, zipper foot No. 4, freehand embroidery foot No. 9, freehand quilting foot No. 29 and ruffler foot No. 86
- *Machine needles*: Size-80 jeans needle
- *Threads*: Mettler poly sheen color 934 fawn and 761 oat
- Mettler pre-wound bobbins
- 15in cushion insert
- Self-adhesive tear-away stabilizer to stabilize embroidery motif
- Stitch-n-tear stabilizer to stabilize machine embroidery stitches
- Water-fading fabric marking pen
- Rotary cutter, quilters ruler and self-healing cutting mat
- Vellum (112gsm) tracing paper
- Tracing paper (dressmakers quality) and lead pencil
- General sewing requirements

* In the customized center block made from the Heart Border Design, to prevent unravelling when cutting the jump stitches, re-digitise the satin stitch to be a step stitch.

CUTTING

1) Use the rotary cutter, quilters ruler and self-healing mat to cut:

From the quilters muslin:

—three, 18in squares—cushion top, lining and backing

—two, 4in strips across the width of the fabric joined to measure 120in for the outside frill

From the satin cut:

—four, 4in squares—for appliqué in the embroidered hearts

—two, 3¼in strips across the width of the fabric joined to measure 120in for the inside frill

From the Vliesofix/Wonderunder cut:

—four, 4in squares to be fused to the back of the matching squares of satin

From the fusible batting cut

—one 18in square to be fused to the back of one of the 18in quilters muslin squares for the top of the cushion.

MARKING THE CUSHION BLOCK

2) Fold one of the 18in quilters muslin squares in half through the center on the vertical, horizontal and diagonal and press.

3) Use the quilting ruler and fabric-marking pen to mark in the folds.

4) Measure out from the center on the diagonal lines 4in and mark this position—center position for the Lacy Heart design.

5) On the same lines measure out from the center 7¾ in and mark this position—center position for the Heart Border design in each corner of the quilt.

DOWN LOADING AND EDITING THE EMBROIDERY MOTIFS

6) Place the Lace and Romantic design CD in the computer and select Twining Guinea Flower design using the Bernina software.

7) **Edit** Twining Guinea Flower in the following way:

—**select** the design by highlighting it (magenta)

—select **Arrange** then **ungroup**

—select center design **Twining Guinea flower delete**

—select **Arrange** menu then select **Auto Center** from the drop down dialog box to center the design. This will enable you to print a template with the cross hairs in the center of the design

—select **Print** and print the design on vellum (112gsm) tracing paper to be used as a template

—select **Save** and name the new design

—select **Write to Machine** on the toolbar to send the new design to the machine to be embroidered.

8) Use the Bernina Artista software to select from **My Designs, Heart Border** design

9) **Edit** Heart Border design in the following way:

—**selec**t the joining stitches and the **heart** in the bottom corner of the design by highlighting it (magenta)

—press **Delete** to delete these stitches

—select **Arrange** menu then select **Auto Center** from the drop down dialog box to center the design. This will enable you to print a template with the cross hairs in the center of the design

—select **Print** and print the design on vellum (112gsm) tracing paper to be used as a template

—select **Save** and name the new design

—select **Write to Machine** on the toolbar to send the new design to the machine to be embroidered.

10) Use the photo and the techniques used in steps No. 8 and No. 9 as a guide to customize the above design to suit the center of the cushion.

Embroidered Hearts

NOTE: *The hearts are embroidered on the diagonal lines. Two have appliqué and two have padded appliqué. Arrange them opposite each other.*

12) Use the heart template centered over the 4in mark on the diagonal lines and mark the center and starting point of the design using the fabric marking pen. (Refer to the techniques section on page 34 for this method)

11) Use the self-adhesive tear-away technique on page 22, size-80 jeans needle, fawn thread, pre-wound bobbins and embroidery foot to embroider the following:

—edited heart as in step No. 7 (Lacy Heart) as an appliqué in each corner on the marked 4in position on the diagonal lines

—Iron Vliesofix/Wonderunder to the back of the four 4in satin squares and fusible batting to the back of two of these squares

—center the padded satin square over the marked position on the diagonal line in the corner of the cushion then go to color No. 2 of the design

—allow the machine to stitch around the edge of the heart with a zig zag stitch using fawn thread. Then stop the machine, remove the hoop from the machine and carefully cut around the edge of the satin fabric close to the row of stitching

—go back to color No. 1, place the hoop back in the machine and stitch the Lacy Heart design omitting the 'net' in the center of the heart

—repeat in the opposite corner of the cushion

—repeat the above embroidered Lacy Heart design in the remaining two corners using the satin with Vliesofix/Wonderunder on the back only, this time stitching the 'net' over the center of the heart appliqué. You may choose to use a thread change for this section of the design.

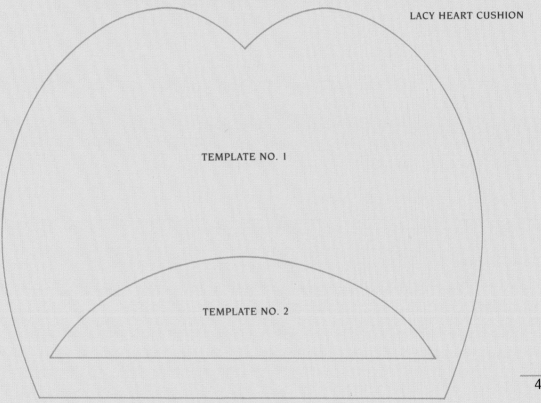

LACY HEART CUSHION

TEMPLATE NO. 1

TEMPLATE NO. 2

41

Edited Corner Designs

12)   Embroider the edited heart border designs using the templates for placement over the 7¾in position marked on the diagonal lines.

TIP: *Ensure your fabric is placed squarely in the hoop, particularly for this design, and aligned on the diagonal lines and square with the corners of the block. It will be very evident if the design is not straight and square as it is a corner design and should be perfectly aligned.*

13)   Embroider the edited Heart Border design in each corner of the cushion using fawn thread for color No. 1 and oat for color No. 2.

Center Design

14) Embroider the customized Heart Border design in the center of the cushion using the above colors.

MACHINE EMBROIDERY STITCHING

15) Use the tracing paper and lead pencil to trace around the templates supplied, then cut them out.

16) Use the photo as a guide to position template No. 1 over the embroidered hearts then use the fabric-marking pen to trace around the template.

17) Use the photo as a guide to position template No. 2 to connect the corner heart embroidery, then use the fabric-marking pen to trace around the template.

18) Use the stitch-n-tear stabilizer at the back of the block, 5mm open toe foot, oat thread, pre-wound bobbin, size-80 jeans needle and stitch No.407 (default width and length) around all the marked templates.

Quilting

19) Pin the second quilters muslin square to the back of the fusible batting.

20) Lower the feed dogs, use the cream polyester thread and the freehand quilting foot to stipple quilt in the arc created by template No. 2 connecting the corner embroidered hearts.

21) Press and trim the cushion block to a 15in square.

Putting it Together

22) Join the frill pieces into a continuous length—one of satin, one of muslin.

23) Use the serger and the three-thread rolled hem to hem the edges of the frills with cream thread.

24) Use the ruffler foot to gather up the frills to fit the cushion and join into a continuous loop then place the satin frill over the muslin frill aligning the raw fabric edges, right side up of both frills and use the standard foot to stitch the frills together close to the row of gathering.

25) Pin, then stitch the frill to the outside edge of the cushion with the right sides of the frill and the cushion together and the raw fabric edges aligned using the standard foot and cream thread.

26) Complete the cushion by inserting the zip in the back of the cushion fabric then placing the right side of the cushion back (leave zip partially open) over the right side of the cushion (frills facing the center of the cushion) and stitching from the wrong side of the fabric around the four sides of the cushion.

27) Turn to the right side and fill with a cushion insert to complete the cushion.

Having developed a taste for *latte* through the Lacy Heart Cushion, now you can explore the wider reaches of creativity with the full *Latte Quilt* project.

The Bernina Latte Quilt

The Bernina Latte Quilt

The Bernina Latte Quilt has been designed as a whole quilt but also so that its parts, such as a single block or the center medallion, can be made separately as a cushion or pillow, as a tablecloth or wall hanging. The techniques for embellishment would work very well on clothing.

You will feel the joy of creative expression and grow in skills and confidence as you sip your coffee while journeying through the Latte Quilt experience.

Note: *In keeping with quilting traditions imperial measurements are used throughout.*

Finished size of Quilt 91½in square

Finished size of Center Medallion 44¼in square

Finished size of Center Block 22½in square

Finished size of Center Block plus triangle grids on point 31½in square

Finished size of Blocks 14in square

Finished size of Borders 5½in

Finished size of Sashing 1¾in

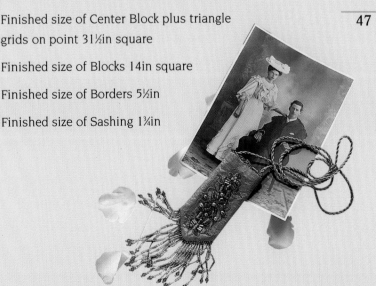

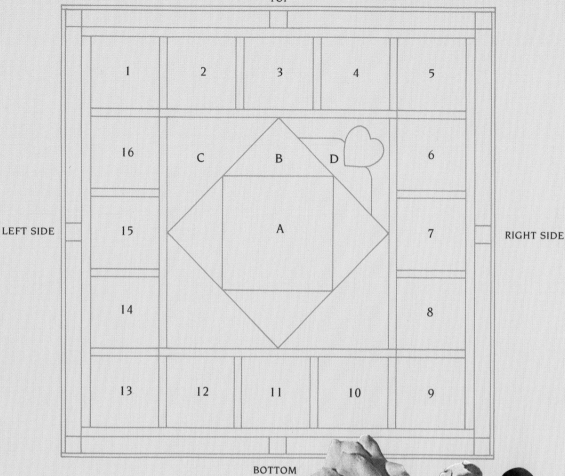

LATTE QUILT LAYOUT

TOP

| 1 | 2 | 3 | 4 | 5 |

| 16 | C | B | D | 6 |

LEFT SIDE

| 15 | A | 7 |

RIGHT SIDE

| 14 | 8 |

| 13 | 12 | 11 | 10 | 9 |

BOTTOM

Materials for Completed Quilt

FABRIC REQUIREMENTS

- 3⅜yd quilters muslin 60in wide
- 6⅜yd Duchess satin 60in wide
- 20 yd fusible batting H640 by Freudenberg
- 3¾yd Jenny Beyer's 110in-wide quilt backing fabric
- 1yd Vliesofix/Wonderunder double-sided fusible web
- 20in Stitch 'n' tear stabilizer for machine fancy stitching
- 1 roll of self-adhesive tear-away sticky-backed stabilizer for hoop embroidery
- 12in Aqua film soluble stabilizer (water-soluble fabric)
- 12in nylon netting

MACHINE AND ASSOCIATED EQUIPMENT

- Bernina Artista 170/180
- Bernina Design software Version 1, 2, or 3 or Bernina Artlink Software
- Bernina CPS software for addition stitches
- Bernina Latte Quilt design CD that accompanies this book
- Artistic Design multi formatted CDs: Beautiful Borders, Artistic Adornments

and Lace and Romantic Designs (optional extra)

- Studio Bernina Beautiful Borders Card No. 527 and Lace and Romantic Designs Card No. 126 for additional designs that go with the *Latte Quilt* (optional extra)

BERNINA FEET AND ACCESSORIES

Standard foot No. 1 for construction and basting

Zipper foot No. 4 for putting in zippers

Darning foot No. 9 for freehand machine embroidery and motif embroidery

Open-toe foot No. 20 for machine embroidery and appliqué

Freehand Quilting foot No. 29 for freehand quilting techniques

Pintuck foot No. 32 for pintucking

Patchwork ¼in foot No. 37 for piecing

Walking foot for quilting and even feeding

Ruffler foot for pleating/ruffling frills

Quilting guide

Second spool holder

Multi-spool holder

Medium and large hoops

Placement grid template for above hoops

Machine needles:

- One packet size-80 jeans needles
- Two 2mm twin needles
- One triple-needle
- One packet hand beading needles
- Long glass headed quilting pins
- Quilters safety pins

Threads:

- Mettler Poly Sheen (Silky Sheen) embroidery thread in the following colors: approx. 10 x 800m reels Fawn No. 934 (853), 10 x 200m Oat No. 761 (761) and 3 x 200m Eggshell No. 101 (670)
- 4 x 800m reels cream Mettler polyester thread for quilting
- 2 reels white Mettler Cordonnet thread for corded pintucks
- Clear beading thread
- 20 pre-wound bobbins for embroidery
- Monofilament thread

Miscellaneous:

- Quilting ruler
- Olfa self-healing cutting mat
- Rotary cutter with new blade
- 15in quilters square
- Quilters tape measure
- Heavy vellum (tracing paper) or quilters template plastic cut to 14½in square

- Vellum (112gsm) tracing paper for printing design templates
- Adhesive spray
- Beads
- Ribbon: 6yd fawn 2mm silk ribbon to twist for tree trunks for the topiary hearts, blocks 7 and 15
- Masking tape and bulldog clips
- Water-soluble fabric-marking pen
- General sewing requirements

Any additional requirements will be given as needed with each section of the quilt.

NOTE: *if you have not already done so it is strongly recommended that you read the Tools of the Trade and Basic Techniques sections of this book before proceeding with the Latte Quilt.*

Cutting

Cut the fabric in the order it is required using a large flat surface and the rotary cutter, mat and quilting ruler. It is of the utmost importance that you are accurate at all times, as the measurements have been calculated to exactly meet the needs of the quilt. It is advisable to check your actual quilt measurements against those given to ensure perfect piecing at all times.

When cutting out, it is a good idea to label the fabric pieces and store them flat in plastic bags to eliminate any excess fraying—especially with the satin.

1. Blocks
2. Center medallion
3. Sashing strips
4. Border and binding strips

Blocks

FROM THE HOMESPUN FABRIC CUT:
—eight, 18in squares. When completed cut to 14½in squares
FROM THE DUCHESS SATIN CUT:
—12, 18in squares—used on the wrong side.
When completed, cut to 14½in squares
—four, 7in squares—used on the right side for the center of corner blocks (No. 1, No. 5, No. 9, and No. 13)
—two, 7in squares—used on the right side for the center of block No. 7 and No. 15. After twin-needle work, cut to 5in squares

—one, 10in x 12in rectangle used to embroider the Flowerpot design
for block No. 7 and No. 15

FROM THE FUSIBLE BATTING CUT:

—20, 18in squares

FROM THE VLIESOFIX/WONDERUNDER CUT:

—four, 7in squares ironed to the back of the matching satin squares
so shiny side is up

—one, 5in square (block No. 7 and No. 15) do not iron to matching
squares until the twin-needle stitching is complete

Marking the blocks

Fold each block (both satin and homespun) first
vertically then horizontally to divide the block through the
center into quarters and press with a steam iron.

Fold the block again on the diagonal to divide the
block into eight equal parts and press.

It is also a good idea to mark the seamlines around
the block as a guide so you do not embroider beyond them.
The finished size of the blocks is 14in, the embroidery will cause some shrinkage
so measure in 1¾in from the cut edge on all sides of the block and draw a square
here by ruling lines parallel to the 18in square.

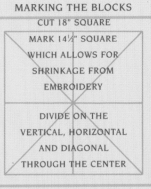

MARKING THE BLOCKS

CUT 18" SQUARE

MARK 14½" SQUARE
WHICH ALLOWS FOR
SHRINKAGE FROM
EMBROIDERY

DIVIDE ON THE
VERTICAL, HORIZONTAL
AND DIAGONAL
THROUGH THE CENTER

NOTE: *Remember that we are using the wrong side of the satin
when folding the blocks.*

51

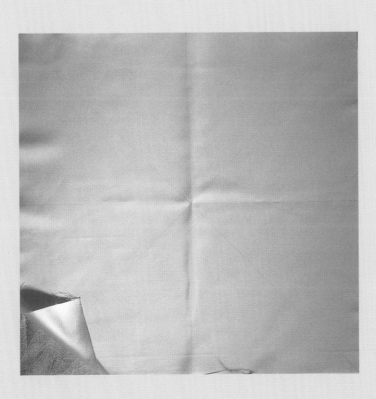

The fold lines on the blocks can either be marked using a water-soluble fabric marking pen or a basting stitch that is easily removed.

It is advisable to test the water-soluble fabric-marking pen to make sure it is easily removed with a light mist of water.

NOTE: *Each block may have additional placement lines marked on it when they are dealt with individually.*

Cutting and Applying the Fabric to be Appliquéd

Using the templates provided and the photographs as a guide, cut out the appliqué pieces for each block and fuse to the designated block using Vliesofix/Wonderunder taking particular care which side of the fabric should be facing up. Specific instructions are included with each block. Refer to the Basic Techniques section on page 28 to apply the Vliesofix/Wonderunder.

DYEING LACE

Should you not have an embroidery machine, lace motifs can be used in place of embroidery motifs, and if necessary dyed to suit. Using a tea/coffee dye gives the best results with colors that blend (quite naturally) with the *Latte Quilt*. Lace to be applied to blocks is placed onto a piece of paper, wrong side up. Over the top of the lace, lay a similar sized piece of Vliesofix/Wonderunder with the paper side up. Iron the Vliesofix/Wonderunder to the lace from the paper side using heat and steam, then allow to cool before removing the backing paper. The excess web sticks to the paper. Peel the lace from the paper, making sure any excess web is pulled away from the outside edge of the lace and in large areas of the lace that are not covered with thread.

TEA/COFFEE DYE RECIPE:
2 tea bags

2 tablespoons of instant coffee

2 tablespoons of vinegar

2 litres/4 pints of boiling water

Boil the above ingredients in a non-reactive saucepan. Drop in lace pieces, Boil for five minutes. Remove from solution with tongs and rinse until clear in cool water. Dry in the shade, pinning out if necessary to keep lace pieces in shape. Press with steam iron when dry.

Machine Stitching

All blocks feature machine embroidery stitches which serve to seal the edges of an appliqué, to connect machine embroidery motifs or to be purely decorative.

This type of embroidery uses a size-80 jeans needle, 40-denier thread in the needle, pre-wound bobbin and either a 5mm or 9mm open-toe foot No. 20 depending on the width of the chosen stitch.

Best match the stitches to those used in each block referring to the photo as a guide to the stitches and thread colors used. This type of stitching requires tear-away stabilizer at the back of the fabric to ensure perfect stitch results.

The entire stabilizer should be removed from the back of the fabric once embroidery is completed.

TIP: *When sewing large scallop designs in small runs, mark the center of the line to be embroidered then sew from this point out to either end to ensure symmetry. You will need to mirror the stitch for one side of the center.*

Motif Embroidery

The *Latte Quilt* CD that accompanies this book has all the embroidery motif designs stored on it that are required to replicate this quilt.
As this CD is multi-formatted, the designs are available to all brands of machines so anyone who has an embroidery machine can create the Bernina *Latte Quilt*.

This type of embroidery also requires stabilizing and unless otherwise directed, use the self-adhesive tear-away in the hoop for ease and accurate placement. Once embroidery is complete the fabric is removed from the stabilizer (not the stabilizer from the hoop) with any excess stabilizer being carefully removed with a small pair of tweezers.

Using the software that is compatible with your machine (remember Bernina has several different versions of software designed to meet the needs of the individual sewer—refer to Tools of the Trade, page 16) transfer the designs from the *Latte Quilt* CD to either a memory card or directly into the sewing machine if you have a Bernina 170/180. If memory capacity of your card/machine does not accommodate all the designs at one time, then do this on a need-to-use basis. The designs needed for each block will be listed at the beginning of the instructions for the individual block.

NOTE: *Do not be discouraged if you do not have access to a machine capable of doing motif embroidery. Use the dyed lace to simulate the embroidery motifs then connect these with stitches best matched to those in the various blocks, referring to the photo as a guide to the stitches and colors used.*

Parasol Block

Blocks No. 1, No. 5, No. 9 and No. 13

Corners

Materials specific to these blocks

🪡 Parasol design from the *Latte Quilt* CD

🪡 *Machine Needles*: 2.0mm twin needle

🪡 Large or medium hoop

🪡 *Machine feet*: standard foot No. 1 and freehand embroidery foot No. 9

🪡 8in square nylon netting (to embroider small flowers over)

🪡 8in square soluble stabilizer to back the above

🪡 CPS software for personal stitch selection

1) Four satin blocks—dull side up used for these blocks.

2) Four 7in satin squares—right side up for the center of the above blocks

3) Use a ruler and fabric-marking pen to plot and draw placement lines for embroidery stitches within and beyond the straight fabric edges of the centre satin square. Draw two squares ½in apart—inside, outside and equidistant from the centre satin square. Then draw another two squares 1¼in apart—inside, outside and equidistant from the center satin square (see labelled photo, page 56).

4) Use template No. 1 to round and cut the corners of the 7in satin squares. Back with Vliesoflix/Wonderunder then iron them to the center of each 18in square on the dull side of the satin (right side of 7in squares uppermost).

Machine Embroidery Stitching

Use the photo as a guide to colors and stitch position and refer to page 103-104 to identify the stitch.

5) Use the open-toe foot and size-80 jeans needle to sew:
—stitch No. 2 (from the machine) (zigzag) width 2.0 density 0.30 using eggshell thread to stitch around the outside edge of the convex curves on the corners of the satin square to appliqué the fabric and seal the edges. Start and finish at each end of the curve.

(a)—stitch from the CPS No. 603 width 9.0 length using fawn thread to stitch along the straight sides of the center satin square to seal the fabric edges.

(b)—stitch from the machine No. 416 width 7.0 density 0.3 using fawn thread in the left and oat in the right of a 2.0mm twin needle to stitch on either side of row (a) on the marked ½in line.

(c)—stitch from the CPS No. 740 width 9.0 length 2.25 using fawn thread to stitch on either side of row (b) on the 1¼ in line.

(d)—stitch from the machine No. 102 default width and length using fawn thread single pattern and securing functions selected to stitch a flower at the 'v' of each scallop on stitch No. 740 row (c).

(e)—stitch from the machine No. 110 default width and length using fawn thread half pattern and securing functions selected sew a leaf starting from the center of the block each time on the four sides of the center on the vertical and horizontal lines. Press pattern start function after each leaf is stitched.

Motif Embroidery

6) Select the parasol placement template and position then mark the block so a parasol will sit over each of the convex corners of the center satin square.

7) Stitch a parasol in a corner of the above using fawn thread.

8) Raise the feed dogs and change to open-toe foot to extend the top of the parasol by ⅝in using fawn thread, stitch No. 2 width 2.0 density 0.3 tapering at the point.

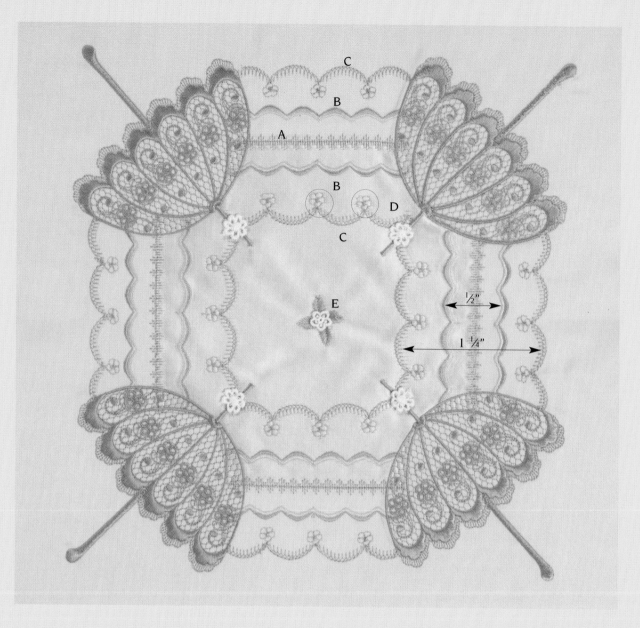

A

B

C

B

D

C

E

½"

1 ¼"

TEMPLATE NO 1
BLOCK NO 1, 5, 9, & 13

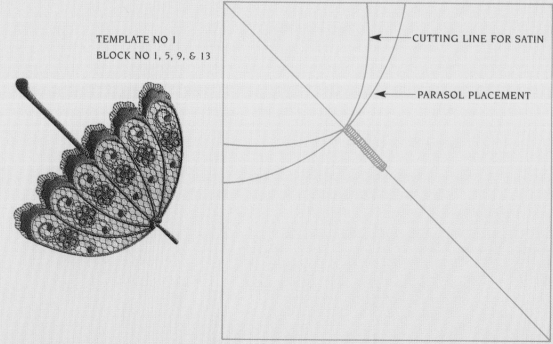

CUTTING LINE FOR SATIN

PARASOL PLACEMENT

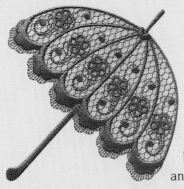

9) Repeat steps 7 and 8 for the remaining three corners of the center satin square.

10) Use the CPS software to select design No. 14 from collection No. 3.

11) Isolate the small daisy from the design then cut and paste it twenty times, these will fit in the medium hoop. Send these to the sewing machine.

12) Hoop the nylon netting over the soluble stabilizer in the medium hoop making sure the fabric is tight in the hoop.Lower the feed dogs and change to freeh and embroidery foot then use eggshell thread to stitch out the daisies.

13) Remove both layers of fabric from the hoop and wash the stabilizer from the back of the netting. Allow to dry flat, then using a small sharp pair of scissors carefully cut each daisy out.

14) Use monofil thread and a freehand straight stitch to stitch the daisies center over the top of each parasol and in the center of each block over the four leaves.

15) Iron the fusible batting to the back of the square and put to one side.

Royal BlueBell Block

Block No. 2 and No. 10

Materials specific to these blocks

- Royal BlueBell design from the *Latte Quilt* CD
- *Machine needles*: Size-80 jeans needle and size-90 embroidery needle
- *Machine feet*: Standard foot No. 1, freehand embroidery foot No. 9, freehand quilt foot No. 29, 9mm open-toe foot No. 20 and 5mm open-toe foot No. 20
- Tracing paper and a lead pencil
- CPS software

1)   Use the quilters' muslin for these two blocks.

Motif Embroidery

2)   Use the size-90 embroidery needle, freehand foot and fawn thread to stitch the Royal BlueBell design.

3)   Select the Royal BlueBell placement template placing it on the top half of the block, centered over the vertical line so each bluebell is centered over the diagonal lines and the 'petals' of the blue bell just touch the vertical and the horizontal lines on the block. Use the fabric–marking pen to mark the center of the design and on either side of the center on the horizontal, then connect these points on the fabric to mark the centering position of the design.

4)   Repeat for the bottom of the block, referring to the photo as a guide.

5)   Embroider both Royal BlueBell designs, centering them. Press the embroidered block over a towel, from the wrong side of the fabric, then iron the fusible batting to the back of the muslin block, taking care not to damage the thread.

Marking the Block

6)   Use the tracing paper and a lead pencil to trace around the templates on page 60, then use paper scissors to cut them out.

7)   Use the photo as a guide to position the templates then use the water-soluble fabric-marking pen to draw around the templates making sure they do not extend beyond the marked seam line on the block.

8)   Measure in and mark 2in from the seam lines on the block on all sides and draw another square. Do not worry if this new square dissects the positions marked above as the lines will be removed when embroidery is complete.

Machine Embroidery Stitches

9)   **Template No. 1**—stitched in fawn colored thread using the 5mm open-toe foot and size-80 jeans needle

       —stitch No. 309 width and length 4.0 sewn over the marked line

       —stitch No. 732 (selected from the CPS) width 3.0 length 1.25 sewn on the outside edge of the previous row so the points of the scallops just touch stitch No. 309

10)   **Template No. 2**—stitched in oat colored thread

       —repeat stitches as for template No. 1

11)   Select fawn colored thread using the standard sewing foot to sew:

       —stitch No. 702 width 3.0 length 3.5 select needle down and sew along the square marked in step No. 8 starting and finishing at template No. 3 line, tying off at the beginning and end of the row using the knee lift to pivot at the corner.

12) **Template No. 3**—stitched in fawn thread using the 5mm open-toe foot

—stitch No. 309 width 3.0 length 3.5 sewn over the marked line

—stitch No. 2 (zigzag) width 1.5 density 0.3 sewn on either side of the above stitch closely aligned with the edges of the stitch.

—stitch 732 (selected from the CPS) default width and length change to the 9mm open-toe foot sewing scallops as for template No.1 and No. 2.

Freehand stipple-quilting

The stipple quilting can be done using the 'quilt-as-you-go' technique by stipple quilting the designated areas of the quilt, block by block, or when the quilt is complete, to hold the quilt layers together—this is your choice.
The instructions are the same for each technique except one is for the block and the other is done through all three layers once the quilt is pieced.

12) Use the freehand quilting foot, lower the feed dogs and use cream polyester thread to stipple-quilt:

—the center area of the block framed by the Royal BlueBell embroidery
—the area inside template No. 2 bordered with the oat colored thread.

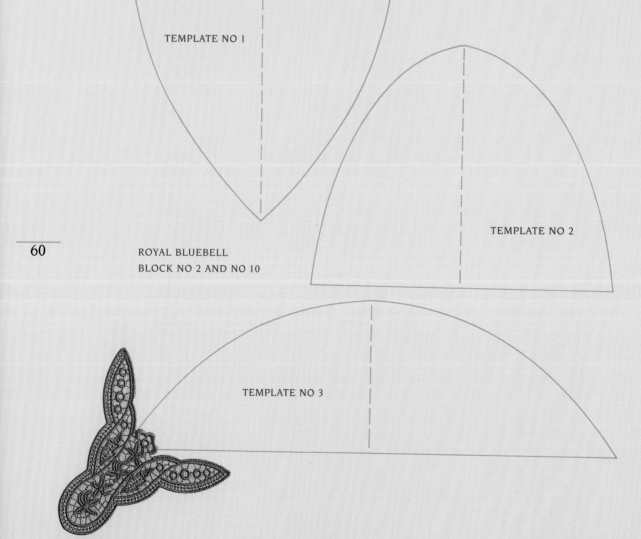

TEMPLATE NO 1

TEMPLATE NO 2

ROYAL BLUEBELL
BLOCK NO 2 AND NO 10

TEMPLATE NO 3

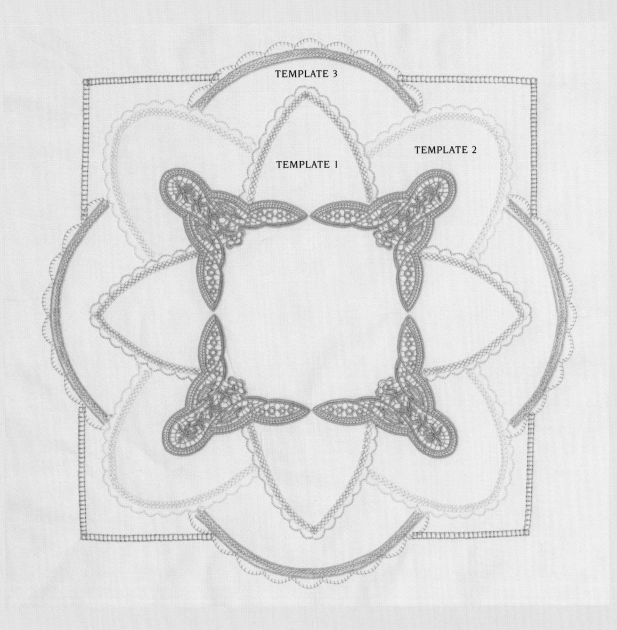

TEMPLATE 3

TEMPLATE 1

TEMPLATE 2

Rambling Rose Block

Block No. 3 and No. 11

Materials specific to these blocks

- NewRamRose design from the *Latte* Quilt CD
- *Machine needles*: Size-80 jeans needle and 2.0mm twin needle
- *Machine feet*: Standard foot No. 1, freehand embroidery foot No. 9, freehand quilting foot No. 29, 5mm open-toe foot No. 20 and 9mm open-toe foot No. 20
- Tracing paper and lead pencil
- CPS software

1)   Use the satin on the wrong side for these two blocks.

Marking the blocks

2)   On diagonal line from the top right corner to the bottom left corner measure out from the center in both directions 1⅞in and mark using a water-soluble fabric-marking pen. (The distance between these two marks should measure 3¾in.)

3)   On the opposite diagonal line (top left corner to bottom right corner) measure out 4in from the center in both directions and mark using a water-soluble fabric marking pen. (The distance between these two marks should measure 8in.)

4)   Place the NewRamRose template supplied over the marked position in step 2 so the center vertical line on the template sits over the diagonal line on the block and the rose faces to the outside of the block. **The bottom 'v' of the scallop should just touch the marked 1⅞in position on the diagonal line**. With the template in this position and using the fabric-marking pen, mark the center of the design and either side of this point. Repeat for the other side of this line. You may also choose to mark the starting point for these designs.

5)   Place the NewRamRose template over the marked position in step 3 so the center vertical line on the template sits over the diagonal line on the block and the rose faces to the center of the block. The top petal of the rose should just touch the 4in position on the diagonal line. With the template in this position and using the fabric-marking pen mark the center of the design and either side of this point. Repeat for the other side of this line. You may also choose to mark the starting point for these two designs.

Embroidery Motifs

6)   This design has two color changes; color 1 is oat and color 2 is fawn. Select a size-90 embroidery needle and the freehand embroidery foot to stitch the Rambling Rose design four times in the marked positions on the block.

7)   Remove stabilizer from the back of the block then press over a towel from the wrong side of the fabric.

8)   Iron the fusible batting to the back of the fabric being careful not to damage the embroidery on the front of the block.

63

Marking the Templates

9)   Use the tracing paper and lead pencil to trace the templates from those on page 64 then use the paper scissors to cut them out.

10) Use the photo as a guide to position then mark around the templates with a fabric-marking pen:

—template 1 connects the Rambling Rose designs facing to the outside of the block

—template 2 sits inside the above Rambling Rose design connecting two outside roses with an arch

—template 3 creates rounded corners for the whole design.

—template 4 links the rounded corners with four arched side segments.

Embroidery Stitches

11) Select a size-80 jeans needle and fawn thread to stitch:

—stitch No. 431 (from the CPS) width 5.0 length 1¼mm using the single pattern and needle down default and the 5mm open-toe foot to stitch around the curves made by the templates. Sew this stitch centered over all the marked template lines.

—stitch No. 135 (from the CPS) default width and length around the inside of template No. 1 and the two portions of template No. 3 above the Rambling Rose embroidery motifs that face to the outside edge of the block, using the width of the 9mm open-toe foot as a guide.

Twin needle grid quilting

Use the photo as guide to the quilted grid position.

12) Place the 2.0mm twin-needle in the machine and thread the needles with the oat thread using the standard foot and quilting guide and a straight stitch to sew a grid of lines ¾in apart, on the vertical and horizontal.

13) Start the quilting on the center vertical marked line on the block, starting and finishing each row of quilting at the embroidery, pulling the threads to the back and tying off after each row of stitching.

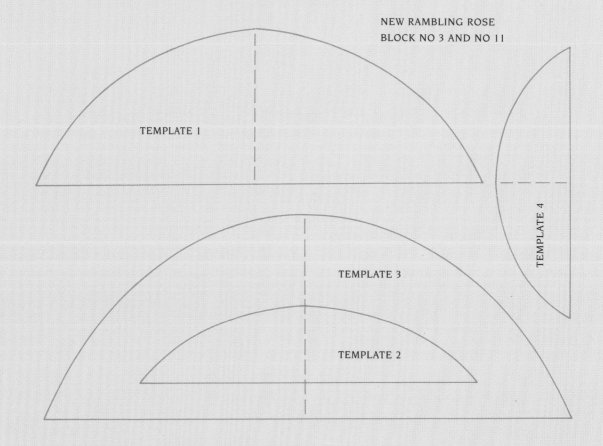

NEW RAMBLING ROSE
BLOCK NO 3 AND NO 11

TEMPLATE 1

TEMPLATE 4

TEMPLATE 3

TEMPLATE 2

Freehand stipple-quilting

The stipple quilting can be done using the 'quilt-as-you-go' technique by stipple quilting the designated areas of the quilt, block by block. Alternatively, it can be done once the quilt is complete to hold the quilt layers together—this is your choice. The instructions are the same for each technique except one is for the block and the other is done once the quilt is pieced through all three layers of the quilt.

14) Use the freehand quilting foot, lower the feed dogs and use cream polyester thread to stipple-quilt:

—the area above the NewRamRose embroidery motifs that face to the outside of the block between the stitching around template No. 2 up to stitch No. 135.

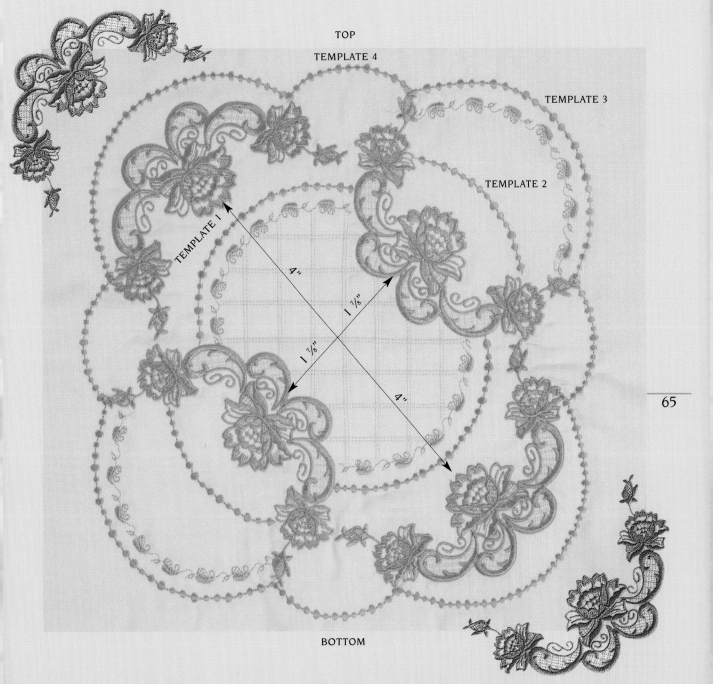

65

Scrolled Border Block

Block No. 4 and No. 12

Materials specific to these blocks

- ScrollB-Cnr design from the *Latte Quilt* CD
- *Machine needles*: Size-80 jeans needle
- *Machine feet*: Standard foot No. 1, freehand embroidery foot No. 9 5mm open-toe foot No. 20 freehand quilting foot No. 29 and 9mm open-toe foot No. 20
- Large Hoop
- Tracing paper and pencil
- Paper scissors
- CPS software

1)   Use the quilters muslin for these two blocks.

Marking the blocks

2)   On the vertical line that divides the block, measure and mark, with a water-soluble fabric-marking pen, 2¾in on either side of the center of the block.

3)   On the horizontal line that divides the block, measure and mark, with a water-soluble fabric-marking pen, 3½in on either side of the center of the block.

4)   Use a fabric marking pen and ruler to mark lines that are parallel to the cut edge of the block and pass through these points forming a rectangle.

5)   Where these lines meet the diagonal lines is the center position for the Scrolled Border embroidery motif design.

6)   Position the ScrollB-Cnr template supplied (design already enlarged refer step 9) over the diagonal lines so the center vertical line marked on the template sits over the marked diagonal line on the block, centered over each corner of the previously marked rectangle.

7)   Use the fabric-marking pen to draw the center horizontal line passing through the diagonal lines at each corner of the rectangle.

8)   This gives centering positions for the Scrolled Border design.

Motif Embroidery

9)   ScrollB-Cnr design needs to be increased in size to fit the block. Use the software to increase/machine to increase the size of ScrollB-Cnr to 3.69in height and 5.07in width, then save the design with a new name.

10)   Use the freehand embroidery foot; size-80 jeans needle, large hoop and fawn thread to stitch the ScrollB-Cnr designs in each corner of the rectangle marked on the block.

TIP: *Take note of the direction you wish the design to sew in and adjust if necessary before sewing. Also check the template placement for each new design to decrease the risk of a galloping incremental error.*

SCROLLB-CNR
BLOCK NO 4 AND NO 12

TEMPLATE 3

TEMPLATE 2

TEMPLATE 1

67

11) Use the CPS collection No. 5, design No. 8 and transfer this design to the sewing machine/card.

12) Select 'auto center' function on the computer then print a template of the design on the vellum (112gsm) tracing paper. Mark the center of the design with vertical and horizontal lines that intersect in the center of the design. Punch holes in the center of the design and on the ends of the vertical and horizontal lines to be used for placement lines marked on the fabric block.

13) Center the above template of design No. 8 on the top and bottom horizontal lines of the marked rectangle so the leaves on the design sit on either side of the center vertical line. Use the water-soluble fabric-marking pen to mark this position,

14) Stitch this design on the above marked positions with the following thread color changes:
   - Color No. 1 Fawn
   - Color No. 2 Oat
   - Color No. 3 Fawn
   - Color No. 4 Eggshell

15) Select the Jenny Haskins Curlicue from the Latte Quilt CD and place the template provided of this design, in between the scrolled border designs on the left and right of the block. Use the photo as a guide for positioning then stitch out using oat thread.

Machine embroidery stitches.

16) Use the tracing paper and lead pencil to trace around then cut out the templates provided.

17) Use the photo as a guide to place the templates then use the fabric marking pen to draw around all templates making sure the curves start and finish in the same place on the embroidery motif on either end of the curves.

18) Select the 5mm open-toe foot, size-80 jeans needle, fawn thread and stitch No. 2 width between 2.0mm and 2.5mm.

19) Satin stitch around all the marked curves using the needle down function and the knee-lift to pivot around the curves.

20) From the machine select stitch No. 708 default width and length then use the 9mm open-toe foot to sew around the outside edge of stitch in step No. 19 so it just touches the edge of the stitch. Using the needle down function and knee lift and pivoting after each stitch ensures perfect stitching.

Freehand stipple-quilting

The stipple quilting can either be done using the 'quilt-as-you-go' technique by stipple quilting the designated areas of the quilt, block by block, or done later when the quilt is complete to hold the quilt layers together—this is your choice. The instructions are the same for each technique except one is for the block and the other is done through all three layers of the quilt once the quilt is pieced.

21)   Use the freehand quilting foot, lower the feed dogs and use cream polyester thread to stipple-quilt:

NOTE: *The small center square formed by the intersecting curves is not stipple-quilted.*

      —on the horizontal shape formed by the machine embroidery stitches, up to and on the other side of the curlicue embroidery design

      —on the vertical shape formed by the machine embroidery stitches up to the inside edge of the oval that frames the CPS embroidery design No. 8.

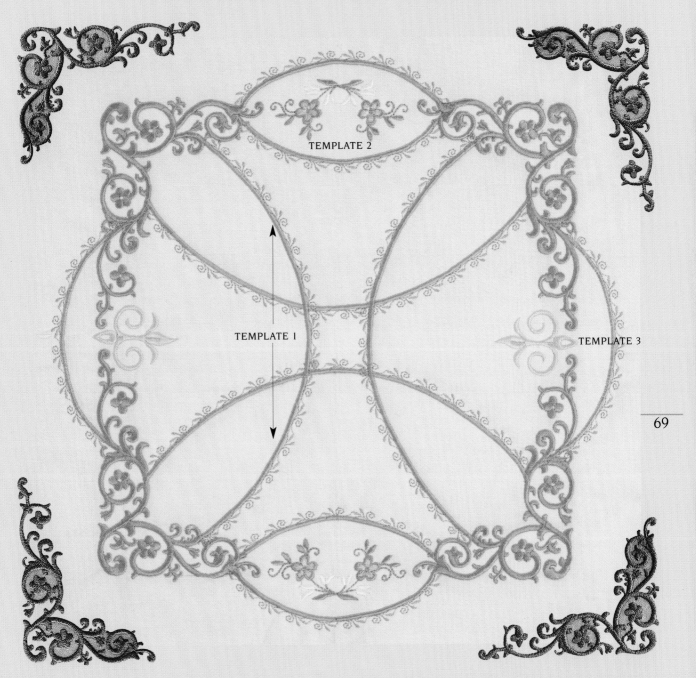

TEMPLATE 2

TEMPLATE 1

TEMPLATE 3

Kashan Braid Block

Block No. 6 and No. 14

Materials specific to these blocks

- 🦢 KashanCentre and HeartKashan designs* from the *Latte Quilt* CD

- 🦢 *Machine needle*: Size-80 jeans needle

- 🦢 *Machine feet*: Standard foot No. 1, freehand embroidery foot No. 9, freehand quilting foot No. 29 and 5mm open-toe foot No. 20

- 🦢 Large hoop

- 🦢 Paper scissors

- 🦢 Tracing paper and lead pencil

* The ART format suits the larger designs. In SEW format with its smaller hoop, improvise by scaling down designs and 'stretching out' connecting elements to embroider the block. Or divide a large design and stitch it out in sections.

1) Use the quilters muslin for these blocks

Motif Embroidery

2) Use the freehand embroidery foot; size-80 jeans needle and the large hoop to stitch the embroidery motifs on these blocks.

3) Use the KashanCentre template provided to place over the muslin square so the center of the design sits over the center of the block and the 'fingers' of the design sit over the diagonal lines, and mark positioning lines on the block.

4) Stitch out the design. There are two colors in this design, use fawn for color No. 1 and oat for Color No. 2.

5) Place the HeartKashan template provided over the diagonal lines on the muslin block so the bottom point of the heart just touches the top of the KashanCentre (heart facing to the outside of the block) and mark positioning lines and starting point of the design on the block.

6) KashanCentre design is sewn out in three colors:
   - Color No. 1 Fawn
   - Color No. 2 Oat
   - Color No. 3 Eggshell

7) Sew HeartKashan on the marked positions on the diagonal lines using the same threads as in step No. 6, in the four corners of the block with the heart facing out to the corner.

8) Press the block over a towel from the wrong side of the fabric.

9) Fuse the batting to the back of the block using a hot steam iron.

Marking the blocks

10) Use the tracing paper and a lead pencil to trace around the templates No.1, 2 and 3 provided here, then use the paper scissors to cut them out.

11) Use the photo as a guide and the fabric-marking pen to trace around templates. Template No. 1 connects the flowers on either side of the heart, template No. 3 connects the buds on either side of the heart and template No.2 is centered over the embroidered hearts in each corner-connecting template No. 3.

Machine embroidery stitches

12) From the stitches in the machine select the 5mm open-toe foot, size 80 jeans needle, stitch No. 407 width 4.0 and length 0.25 and fawn thread to sew around template No. 1.

13) From the stitches in the machine select stitch No. 117 default width and length and fawn thread to stitch around template No. 2 and No. 3 so the stitching flows as one continuous line, using the single pattern and needle

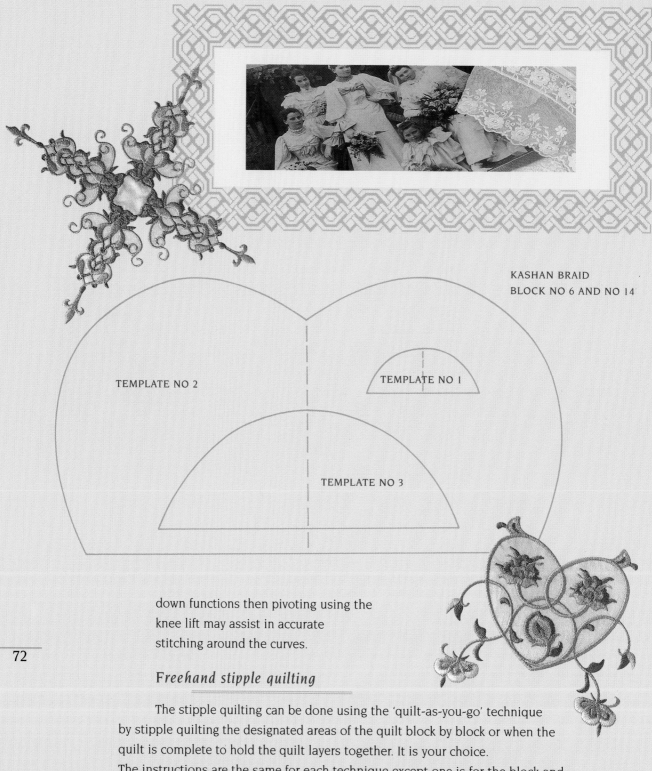

KASHAN BRAID
BLOCK NO 6 AND NO 14

TEMPLATE NO 2

TEMPLATE NO 1

TEMPLATE NO 3

down functions then pivoting using the
knee lift may assist in accurate
stitching around the curves.

Freehand stipple quilting

The stipple quilting can be done using the 'quilt-as-you-go' technique
by stipple quilting the designated areas of the quilt block by block or when the
quilt is complete to hold the quilt layers together. It is your choice.
The instructions are the same for each technique except one is for the block and
the other is done once the quilt is pieced through all three layers of the quilt.

14)   Use the freehand quilting foot, lower the feed dogs and use cream
       polyester thread to stipple-quilt:

       —all areas in and around the embroidery except over the top of the hearts
       under template No. 2.

TEMPLATE 3

TEMPLATE 2

TEMPLATE 2

TEMPLATE 1

TEMPLATE 3

TEMPLATE 1

TEMPLATE 1

TEMPLATE 3

TEMPLATE 1

TEMPLATE 2

TEMPLATE 2

TEMPLATE 3

Topiary Hearts

Block No 7 and No 15

Materials specific to these blocks

- Flowerpot design from the *Latte Quilt* CD

- Two, 8in squares of satin for twin needle work cut to 5in after stitching

- Two, 5in squares of Vliesofix/Wonderunder to iron to the above after cutting

- 10in x 12in piece of satin to embroider pots on

- Two, 11in x 13in pieces of nylon netting to embroider pansy hearts

- Three, 11in x 13in pieces of Aqua film to stabilize the netting

- 6yd fawn 2mm silk ribbon to twist for tree trunks

- *Machine needles*: Size-80 jeans needle, size-90 embroidery needle and 2.0mm twin needle

- *Machine feet*: Standard foot No 1, freehand embroidery foot No 9, pintuck foot No 32, 5mm open-toe foot No 20 and 9mm open-toe foot No 20
- One reel white Cordonnet thread for cording pin tucks
- Monofilament thread
- Small glass beads
- Beading needle and thread
- Large hoop
- CPS software
- 4in x 2¼in piece of cardboard for making 'Mondo grass'

1) Use the satin squares wrong side up for these blocks.

Marking the blocks

2) On the wrong side of the two 8in squares of satin draw a diagonal grid with the lines ¾in apart. Start from the center—corner to corner.

Corded pintucks

3) Thread the 2.0mm twin needle with fawn thread through both needles, pintuck foot and a straight stitch. Refer to the techniques section on page 30 for corded pintucks using the Cordonnet thread.

4) Pintuck from the wrong side of the satin along the marked grid lines on both pieces of 8in squares of satin.

5) When complete, iron from the wrong side of the satin (pintucked side) then cut the squares to 5in and iron the matching Vliesofix/Wonderunder to the wrong side—dull side of the satin. The shiny side—right side of the fabric with the underside of the pintucks is the right side of the fabric.

6) Fuse this square, shiny side up, to the center of both 18in satin squares on the dull side of the satin.

Machine stitching

7) Use the size-80 jeans needle, 5mm open-toe foot and fawn thread to sew stitch No. 2 width 2.0mm and density 0.30 to stitch over the raw edges of the Pintucked Square in the center of the block.

8) Select stitch No 117 default width and length using fawn thread over the above row of stitching as a decorative finish to the Pintucked Square.

Motif Embroidery

9) Use the CPS software to select design No 965016 from the Medley collection, reduce size to height 2.41in, width 2.42in then use software to duplicate the design four times in the one frame and transfer the design to the sewing machine. Embroider eight pansy hearts for the two blocks.

10) Place the netting and layers of Aqua film very tightly in the large hoop together with the netting over the film.

11) Embroider the eight hearts using the following color changes:
   - ✂ Color No 1 Oat
   - ✂ Color No 2 & 3 Eggshell
   - ✂ Color No 4 & 5 Fawn

12) When the embroidery is complete remove the netting and Aqua film from the hoop and soak in warm water to remove the soluble stabilizer. Carefully cut out the pansy hearts. You may choose to use a stencil iron to melt any netting that has not been cut away from around the edge of the hearts.

13) Select the Flowerpot design from the *Latte Quilt* CD and arrange it to fit eight times in the large hoop before sending it to the machine.

TIP: *You may need to either tighten your bobbin tension or loosen your upper tension when stitching out this design to ensure the bobbin thread is not seen from the top of the embroidery.*

14) Use oat colored thread to stitch the Flowerpot designs on the 10in x 12in satin fabric.

15) Use a small sharp pair of scissors to carefully cut around the outside edge of each design, close to the row of outside stitching.

16) Pin the pansy hearts over each corner of the pintucked satin square centered on the diagonal lines.

Twisted Ribbon tree trunks

See Basic Techniques page 35

17) Use 2½in of twisted cord for each trunk, tying off at each end before cutting the cord.

18) Lay the twisted cord along the diagonal line so one knotted end is hidden under the point of the embroidered heart and pin.

19) Use the freehand embroidery foot, size-80 jeans needle, monofilament thread and a straight stitch to sew:

—around the outside and inside edge of the embroidered heart sitting over the knotted end of the twisted ribbon trunk securing both in place

—down the center of the twisted ribbon sitting over the diagonal line to hold the tree trunk in place

Mondo Grass

See Basic Techniques page 35 and make eight pieces of Mondo grass.

Putting it all together

20) Place then pin the Mondo grass behind each pot, with ⅜in of grass showing above the pot. Secure the Mondo grass in place with a zigzag stitch width 2.0 density 0.5 down the center of the pot, using monofilament thread, feed-dogs up and the 5mm open-toe foot.

21) Pin the pots over the other end of the twisted ribbon (over the knot) so the ends of the Mondo grass are approximately 1½in down from the pointed end of the heart.

22) Use the freehand embroidery foot, size-80 jeans needle, monofilament thread and a straight stitch to sew around the edge of the pot securing it in place. (The Mondo grass is free-standing over the twisted ribbon tree trunk.)

Beading

31) Use the beads, beading needle and thread to hand sew the beads in the center of each flower in the topiary heart and on every intersecting line on the corded pin tuck grid to complete the block.

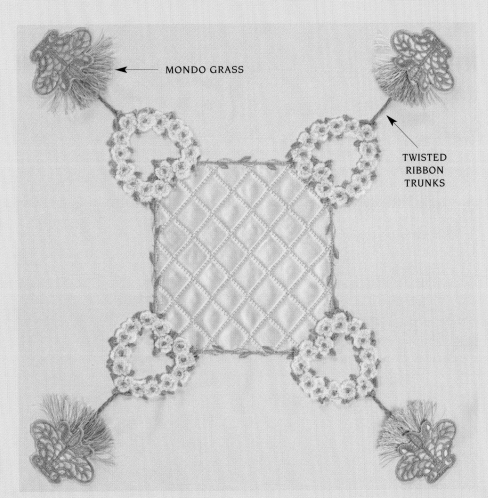

MONDO GRASS

TWISTED RIBBON TRUNKS

Kashan Florence Corner Block

Block No 8 and No 16

Materials specific to these blocks

- Kashan2Florence design and Florence1x3a and Florence1x3b design from the *Latte Quilt* CD

- *Machine needles:* Size-80 jeans needle

- *Machine feet:* Freehand embroidery foot No 9, freehand quilting foot No 29, and 9mm open-toe foot

- Large hoop

- Tracing paper and lead pencil

- Paper scissors

1) Use the quilters muslin for these blocks.

Marking the blocks

2) From the center measure out 3⅜in on either side on the vertical and horizontal lines and mark this position using a water-soluble fabric-marking pen. This is the center position for the Kashan2Florence design.

3) From the center measure out 6⅜in on either side on the diagonal lines and mark this position using a water-soluble fabric-marking pen. This is the center position for the Florence1 design.

Motif Embroidery

4) Use the template provided of Kashan2Florence and place it over the 3⅜in marked position on the vertical and horizontal lines, so the design faces to the outside of the block and use the fabric-marking pen to mark the placement position for this design.

5) Select the freehand embroidery foot, size-80 jeans needle and Kashan2Florence design to stitch centered over the above marked lines. There are three colors changes in this design:
- Color No 1 Fawn
- Color No 2 Eggshell
- Color No 3 Oat

6) Use the software/machine to increase the size of Florence1x3a and Florence1x3b to a height of 2.08in and the width to 1.89in, which fits the finished design better.

7) Use the template provided (design already enlarged) of Florence1x3a/3b and place it over the 6⅜in marked position on the diagonal lines in each corner and the center of the block. Mark the placement position for this design using a fabric-marking pen.

8) Sew Florence1x3b in the center and two opposite corners using the following thread color changes:
- Color No 1 Fawn
- Color No 2 Eggshell
- Color No 3 Fawn
- Color No 4 Oat

9) Sew Florence1x3a in the remaining two opposite corners using the following thread color changes
- Color No 1 Fawn
- Color No 2 Oat
- Color No 3 Eggshell
- Color No 4 Fawn

10) Press the embroidered block from the wrong side over a towel using a hot steam iron, then fuse the wadding to the back of the block.

Embroidery stitching

11) Use the tracing paper and pencil to trace around the shaping templates provided, then use the paper scissors to cut these out. Use a fabric-marking pen to trace around the shaping templates on the block in the following positions:

—shaping template No 2 (convex curve) connects the baskets in the center of the block

—shaping template No 1 forms a handle around the top of the basket

12) Use the size-90 embroidery needle, 9mm open-toe foot and oat thread and from the machine select stitch No 407 width 6.0mm and length 0.25 to stitch around all template lines.

Freehand stipple quilting

The stipple quilting can be done either using the 'quilt-as-you-go' technique by stipple quilting the designated areas of the quilt, block by block, or when the quilt is complete to hold the quilt layers together. This is your choice. The instructions are the same for each technique except one is for the block and the other is done through all three layers of the quilt after the quilt is pieced.

13) Use the freehand quilting foot, lower the feed dogs and use cream polyester thread to stipple-quilt:

—the area in the center of the quilt framed by template No 2 and the baskets.

KASHAN FLORENCE CORNER
BLOCK NO 8 AND NO 16

TEMPLATE NO 1

TEMPLATE NO 2

TEMPLATE 1

TEMPLATE 2

Center Medallion

NOTE: *It is recommended that the fusible batting be fused to the back of the satin fabric before cutting out the border and sashing strips.*

Refer to the layout diagram No. 1 to identify these pieces

FROM THE SATIN CUT:

(c) —two, 23½in squares (to be used dull side up) each square cut into two triangles, (four triangles in total) on the diagonal for the outside border of center medallion, stitched to either side of (e)

(e) —two, 18½in squares. These squares are triple-needle quilted on the dull side of the satin then each square is trimmed to 16½in then cut in half on the diagonal (four right-angled triangles) to be stitched to the four sides of (f)

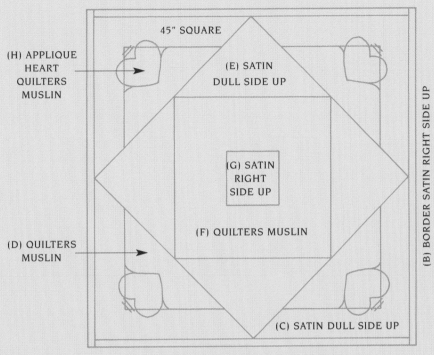

CUTTING DIAGRAM FOR CENTER MEDALLION
DIAGRAM NO 1

45" SQUARE

(H) APPLIQUE HEART QUILTERS MUSLIN

(E) SATIN DULL SIDE UP

(G) SATIN RIGHT SIDE UP

(F) QUILTERS MUSLIN

(D) QUILTERS MUSLIN

(B) BORDER SATIN RIGHT SIDE UP

(C) SATIN DULL SIDE UP

(A) BORDER SATIN RIGHT SIDE UP

(g)   —one, 6in square right side up to be use for appliqué in the center of the homespun block (f)

FROM THE QUILTERS' MUSLIN CUT:

(d)   —two, 17in squares each cut into two triangles (four triangles in total), on the diagonal, to be fused to (c)

(f)   —one, 25in square trimmed to 23in after embroidery center block edged with (e) and having (g) center appliqué edged with embroidery motifs

(h)   —one, 20in square from which the four hearts are cut using the templates provided

FROM THE FUSIBLE BATTING CUT:

—two, 23½in squares to be fused to (c)
—two, 18½in square to be fused to (e) before triple needle quilting
—one, 25in square to be fused to (f)

FROM THE VLIESOFIX/WONDERUNDER CUT:

—two, 17in squares fused to the back of (d)
—one, 20in square fused to the back of (h) then trace out
   four hearts using the template provided and cut the hearts out

NOTE: The Center Medallion will be worked from the center out.

83

(G) TEMPLATE NO 2

11½"

7½" (D) TEMPLATE NO 1

2⅜"

(B) 4

(D) TEMPLATE NO 1

7½" (C) 3

6¼"

(G) TEMPLATE NO 2

(E) TEMPLATE NO 1

(E) TEMPLATE NO 1

11" SQUARE

CENTER POSITION (A)

(E) TEMPLATE NO 1

(B) 2 FLIPPED

2⅜"

(G) TEMPLATE NO 2

(B) 5 FLIPPED

2⅜"

EMBROIDERED SQUARE (A)

(E) TEMPLATE NO 1

(E) TEMPLATE NO 1

6¼" (C) 6

8" (from center to diamond point)

(B) 1

11" SQUARE

7½" (D) TEMPLATE NO 1

7½" (D) TEMPLATE NO 1

2⅜"

13½"

16¼" SQUARE

(F) EMBROIDERY STITCHES

19" SQUARE

(G) TEMPLATE NO 2

(H) STIPPLE QUILTING

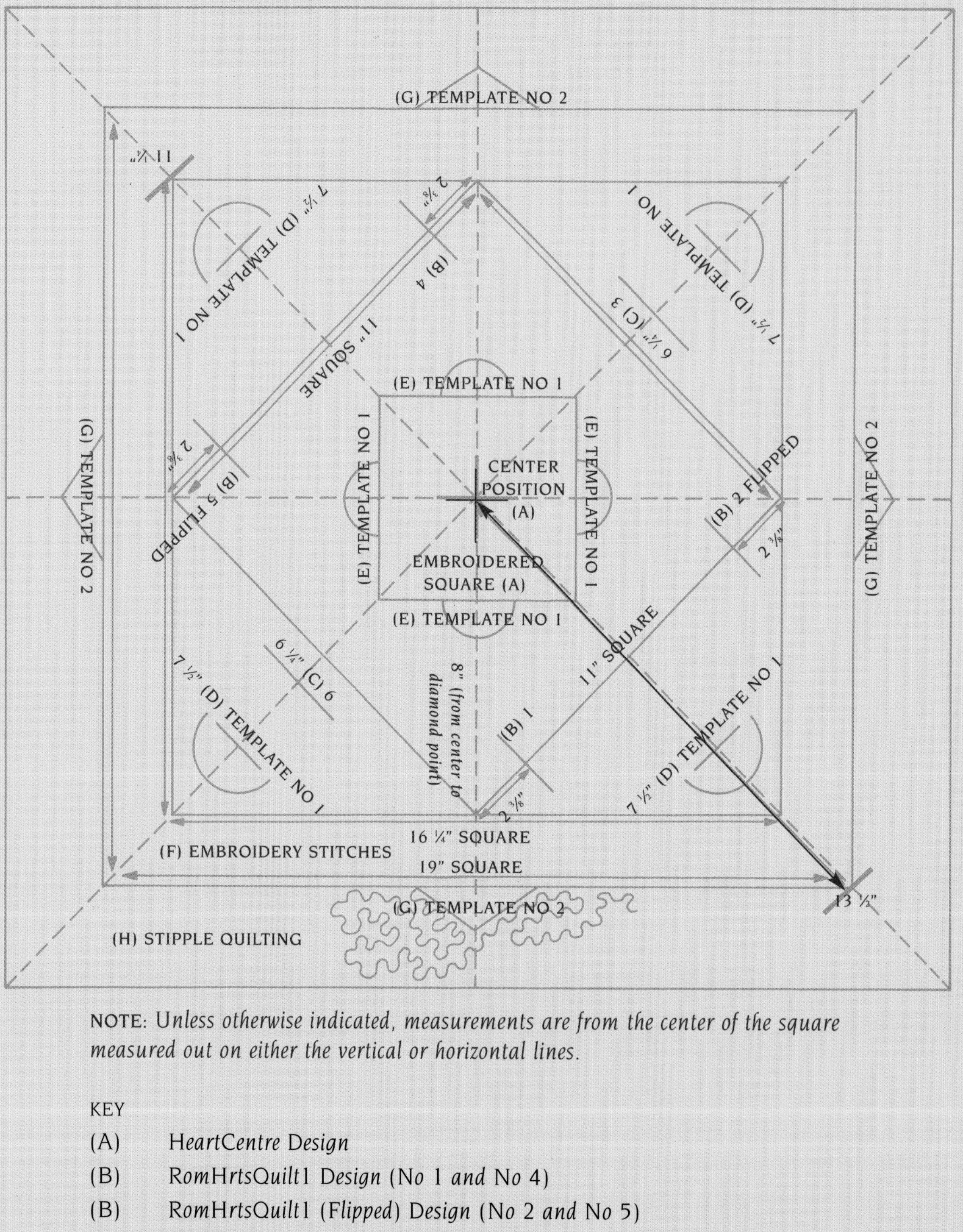

NOTE: *Unless otherwise indicated, measurements are from the center of the square measured out on either the vertical or horizontal lines.*

KEY

(A)   HeartCentre Design

(B)   RomHrtsQuilt1 Design (No 1 and No 4)

(B)   RomHrtsQuilt1 (Flipped) Design (No 2 and No 5)

(C)   RomhrtsQuilt2 Design (No 3 and No 6)

(D)   Florence1x3b enlarged

(E)   Template No 1 on each side of (A) and around (D)

(F)   Stitch No 2 Stitch No 732 (around template No 1)

         Stitch No 2 Stitch No 732 (around 16 ¼in square)

(G)   Template No 2 centered over Vertical and Horizontal lines intersecting 19in square

(H)   Freehand stipple quilting

Center Embroidered Quilters Muslin Square (F)

The center muslin block is dependent on accurate embroidery placement and as it is the focal point of the quilt it is of the utmost importance to make sure all the embroidery positions and lines are accurate. It is a good idea to double check your measurements and make sure all lines intersect through the center of the block, and, when called for, are parallel to the edge of the block.

Marking the center block:

1) Fold (f) the quilters muslin 25in square in half on the vertical and horizontal and then the diagonal from corner to corner and press.
Use either the fabric marking pen or a basting stitch to mark these folds.

TIP: *When marking this block always measure from the center of the block out to ensure the center of the block is maintained. Double-check all measurements making sure they are accurate and match those given.*

2) Measure out from the center then use a ruler and fabric-marking pen to mark: (**Refer to the layout diagram**)

—on each of the diagonal lines, 13½in then connect these points to form a 19in square on the outside of the block. This square forms the boundary for the stipple quilting around the outside edge of the block.

—on each of the diagonal lines, 11¼in then connect these points to form a 16¼in square used as a guide to stitch embroidery stitches over.

—on the vertical and horizontal lines, 8in then connect these points to form an 11in square on point (diamond). This diamond is used to position Romhrtsquilt1 and Romhrtsquilt2 templates over to embroider a square on point (diamond).

Embroidering the Block

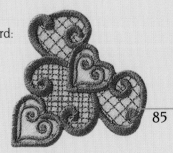

3) From the *Latte Quilt* CD select then download to the machine/card:
—HeartCentre (A) (center of quilt)*
—RomHrtsQuilt1 (B),
—RomHrtsQuilt2 (C), (diamond embroidery around center)
—Florence1x3b (D) (enlarge to 2.08in height and 1.09in width)
(flowers embroidered on the diagonal lines outside edge
of the diamond embroidery).

*Due to the large size of this design, embroidering it in formats other than Bernina's **ART** needs the following modification:
ı) Open the Romantic Heart small corner design and embroider it four times. This will require rotation of the design and re-hooping to create the same effect
   OR
ıı) The design can be duplicated and mirror imaged to create half of the design and then sewn out twice. This will also require re-hooping.

4) Use the **CENTER EMBROIDERED BLOCK LAYOUT** diagram
No. 2 and the templates to mark all embroidery positions and stitch
the embroidery motifs/stitches on the block.

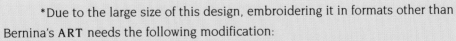

5) Use the templates provided (Florence1x3b has already been enlarged), to place over the center block on the corresponding marked positions and mark the center positions of the designs to be embroidered in sequence on a need-to-use basis. (Too many marks may become confusing.)

6) **HEARTCENTRE (A)**

(i) Fold the 6in satin square in half on the vertical and horizontal through the center then use a ruler and fabric-marking pen to mark these lines.

TEMPLATES FOR CENTER BLOCK

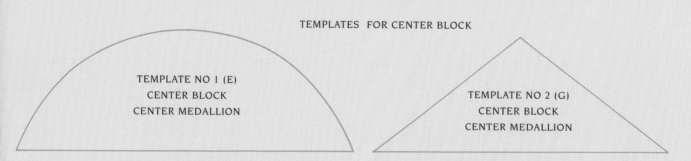

TEMPLATE NO 1 (E)
CENTER BLOCK
CENTER MEDALLION

TEMPLATE NO 2 (G)
CENTER BLOCK
CENTER MEDALLION

(ii) Use basting spray to spray the back of the 6in satin square.

(iii) Match the lines on the satin square with the corresponding lines on the homespun block then press to center of the block to hold it in place.

(iv) Embroider HeartCentre (A) design centered over the satin square in the center of the homespun block in the following sequence and colors:

🧵 Color No. 1 Oat embroider grid, then remove the hoop from the machine to carefully lift the outside of the sprayed square of satin and cut around the outside edge of the grid embroidery. Place hoop back in the machine to embroider:

🧵 Color No. 2 Fawn

7) **DIAMOND EMBROIDERY**

Embroider in an anti-clockwise direction on the 11in square on point:
1. (B) RomHrtsQuilt1
2. (B) RomHrtsQuilt1 Flipped
3. (C) RomHrtsQuilt2
4. (B) RomHrtsQuilt1
5. (B) RomHrtsQuilt1 Flipped
6. (C) RomHrtsQuilt2

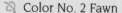

Using the following color sequence:

🧵 Color 1 Fawn

🧵 Color 2 Oat

8) **Embroider the following on the 7½in marked position on the diagonal lines:**

(D) Florence1x3b on diagonal line on the marked position in each corner of the block

🧵 Color 1 Fawn

🧵 Color 2 Eggshell

⊰ Color 3 Fawn
⊰ Color 4 Oat

9) Press the embroidered block over a towel from the wrong side with a hot steam iron then fuse the 25in square batting to the back of the embroidered fabric block.

10) **MACHINE FANCY EMBROIDERY STITCHES (F)**

—use the tracing paper and lead pencil to trace around then cut out the templates supplied

—use the photo as a guide to position then trace around the templates using the fabric-marking pen:

—template No. 1 on each side of embroidery (A)

—template No. 1 on the diagonal lines centered between the points on either side of the line over Florence1x3b (D) embroidery

Use the 5mm/9mm open-toe foot, size-80 jeans needle and fawn thread to sew around all the marked templates and the 16¼in square:

—stitch No. 2 width 2.0 density 0.3 centered templates (D) and (E) around the 16¼in square (5mm open-toe foot)

—stitch No. 732 (selected from the CPS) width 3.0 length 1.25 around the outside edge of stitch No. 2 on template No. 1 (D) and (E) (5mm open-toe-foot)

—stitch 732 (selected from the CPS) default width and length around the outside edge of stitch No. 2 on the 16¼in square using the 9mm open-toe foot.

11) **FREEHAND QUILTING (H)**

12) Lower the feed dogs, use the freehand quilting foot, size-80 jeans needle, cream polyester thread and a straight stitch to:

—stipple-quilt the area between the embroidery and the 16¼in square in each corner

Position template No.2 (G) over the vertical and horizontal lines where they intersect the 19in square referring to the Center Embroidered Block Layout diagram

—stipple-quilt from the raw fabric edges of the block up to the 19in square divided in half by template No.2 (G) aligning the edge of the stippling with the marked lines.

13) Press the embroidered block then, maintaining the center, trim the sides to measure a 23in square. Put to one side.

Triple Needle Quilted Triangles (E)

1) Fuse the matching squares of batting to the 18½in satin squares ironing them to the shiny side of the squares; the dull side is the right side of these squares.

2) Use the triple needle, a straight stitch, the walking foot, the quilting guide, the multi thread stand and fawn through the center needle and oat on

either side needle to quilt a vertical and horizontal grid that is ¾in apart (the quilting guide will give accurately spaced lines). Quilt both blocks.

3) When the quilting is complete, square the blocks then cut each block in half on the diagonal from corner to corner giving four right-angle triangles.

4) Use the beading needle, beads and thread to bead two of the triangles stitching a bead over every intersecting line of the triple needle grid.

5) Put these to one side,

Outer Appliquéd Square and Borders (C overlaid with D)

1) Use the tracing paper and pencil to trace around the heart templates provided on page 90 then cut them out.

2) Fuse the matching squares of batting to the two 23½in squares of satin (c) iron them to the shiny side of the squares; the dull side is the right side of these squares.

3) Cut the above (c) in half on the diagonal to form four equal right-angled triangles.

4) **Iron the Vliesofix/Wonderunder to the:**
—two, 17in squares of quilters muslin (d) to be fused to (c) then cut these squares in half on the diagonal to form four equal right-angled triangles

5) **Use the fabric-marking pen to trace around:**
—heart template four times on (h) making the vertical center line and placement position for the bottom of the pot in the FlorenceNo2 (enlarged) do not cut out

—measure 4in on either side of the right-angled corners on the triangles cut from (d) then round them using a large dinner plate. Sit the plate over the corner of the fabric so the plate touches the 4in marked positions on either side of the corner on (d) then draw around the outside edge of the plate using a fabric-marking pen. Cut around the outside edge of the above curve on each triangle.

6) Center the long side of the muslin triangles (d) over the long side of the satin triangles (c) aligning the cut edges and fusing them together using a hot steam iron.

EMBROIDERING THE CENTER OF THE HEARTS TO BE APPLIQUÉD

7) Select FlorenceNo2 from the *Latte Quilt* CD and enlarge it to a height of 5.02in and width 4.64in then transfer it to the card/machine. Use the template of this design provided (already enlarged), centered on the center vertical line marked on the heart on the quilters muslin, aligning the base of the pot in the FlorenceNo2 design with the marked position on the vertical line and mark the center of the design.

8) Use the freehand embroidery foot and size-80 jeans needle to embroider FlorenceNo2 in the center of the four hearts traced on the quilters muslin to be appliquéd, using the following colors and sequence:
Color No. 1 Fawn

ø Color No. 2 Eggshell

ø Color No. 3 Oat

9) Use a hot steam iron to press the designs over a towel then fuse the matching Vliesofix/Wonderunder square to the back of the muslin.

10) Check the heart template against the traced heart and retrace if necessary as the fabric may have shrunk due to embroidery, then carefully cut out each heart around the traced outline.

Machine embroidery stitching

11) Find the center of the long side of the triangles (c) with the muslin (d) fused to the dull side of the satin and mark this point. Use the fabric marking pen and ruler to draw a straight line that extends from the right-angled corner of (c) to this point. Repeat for the remaining three triangles.

12) Measure out 6¼in from the corner on the above line. Then mark as a reference point to position the top 'v' of the appliqué heart over. Remember to align the bottom 'v' of the heart on the same line to ensure the heart is straight. Iron the four hearts in each triangle over the marked line aligning the top 'v' of the heart with the 6¼in position marked on this line

13) **Use the open-toe foot, size-80 jeans needle and fawn thread to appliqué around the embroidered hearts and the edges of the muslin triangles using:**

—stitch No. 2 width 2.0 density 0.3 over the raw fabric edges

—stitch No. 427 (selected from the CPS) default width and length on the inside of the above stitch

—stitch No. 732 (selected from the CPS) default width and length around the outside edge of the heart only.

Putting it all Together

NOTE: *All seams are ¼in and are stitched using cream construction thread, size-80 jeans needle and the quilters foot/¼in foot for accurate piecing.*

14) Check all measurements against those given in the instructions then make sure all the pieces are cut accurately and pressed.

15) **Stitch the following together:**

—triple-needle quilted triangles (e) to the sides of the embroidered center block (f) forming a square on point

—appliquéd triangles (c) to the sides of (f)

Put to one side.

CENTER MEDALLION
CORNER APPLIQUÉ HEARTS

TRACE ON TO QUILTERS MUSLIN (H)
EMBROIDER AND CUT (4)
HEART TEMPLATE CORNERS
CENTER MEDALLION
PLACE ON FOLD
PLACEMENT POSITION
FOR THE BASE
OF FLORENCENO2
EMBROIDERY DESIGN

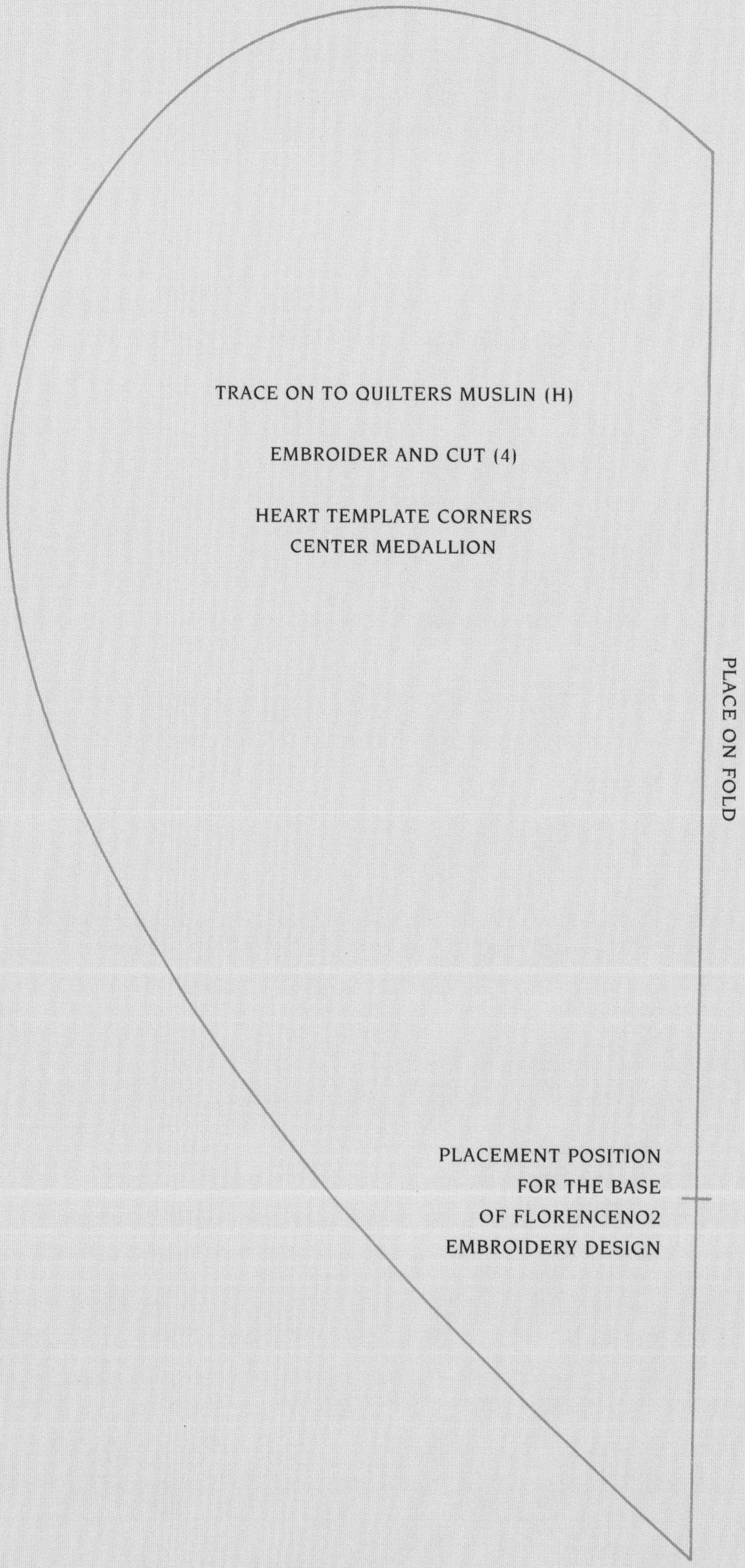

Putting it all Together

Sashing, Borders and Binding

NOTE: It is recommended that the fusible batting be fused to the back of the satin fabric before cutting out the border and sashing strips. **Do not fuse batting to the back of the binding strips or the eight squares that are to be embroidered.**

From the satin cut:

—2in wide strips, right side up across the width of the fabric joined to measure 10½ yards for binding

—two, center medallion (a) border strips 2¼in x 46in satin side up to be stitched to the sides of the center medallion

—two, center medallion (b) border strips 2¼in x 49½in satin side up to be stitched to the top and bottom of the center medallion

—eight, 7in squares, right side up, cut to 5¾in after embroidery for feature and corner blocks in the outside borders

—eight, 5¾in x 36¾in strips, wrong side up, for outside borders

—16, 2¼in x 14½in strips, right sides up, sashing to join blocks into rows

—two, 2¼in x 77½in strips, right side up, inside borders joined to the left and right sides of the quilt

—two, 2¼in x 81in strips, right side up, inside borders joined to the top and bottom of the quilt

From the fusible batting cut:

—eight, 5¾in squares to be fused to the embroidered satin blocks

Squaring the Blocks

1) Use heavyweight vellum tracing paper or template plastic to draw, then cut out, a 14½in square that is divided through the center with vertical and horizontal lines.

2) Place this template over each block matching the marked vertical and horizontal lines then cut each block to 14½in using the template as a guide.

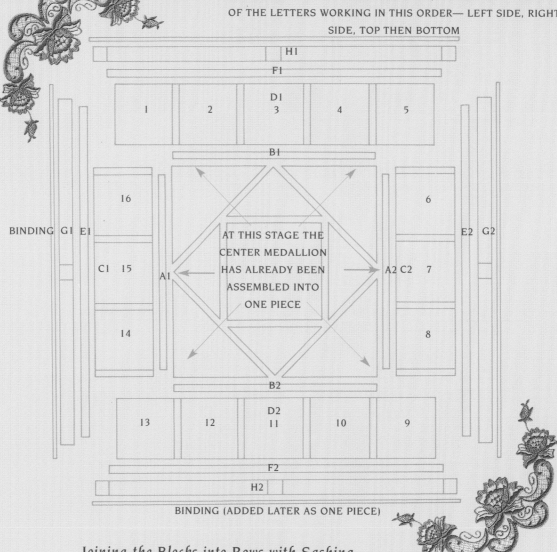

Joining the Blocks into Rows with Sashing

NOTE: *All seams are ¼in and are stitched using cream construction thread,
size-80 jeans needle and the quilters foot/¼in foot for accurate piecing.*

3) Use the assembly layout (above) and the photo on page 46 as a guide to
the block positions, and lay them out on a large flat surface in sequence.

4) Join the blocks together with the 16, 2¼in x 14¼in sashing strips:
Top row: Blocks No. 1–No. 5 starting and finishing with a block
Bottom row: Blocks No. 9–No. 13 starting and finishing with a block
Left hand side row: Blocks No. 14–No. 16 starting and finishing
with sashing
Right hand side row: Blocks No. 6–No. 8 starting and finishing
with sashing

5) Trim the block rows making sure the sides are straight and checking your
measurements against those in the book.

Joining the Center Medallion to the Blocks

6) **Attach the satin borders to the center medallion:**
—two, center medallion (a) border strips 2¼in x 46in satin side up to be
stitched to the sides of the center medallion

—two, center medallion (b) border strips 2¼in x 49½in satin side up to be stitched to the top and bottom of the center medallion

7) Stitch the left hand row (Block No. 14–No. 16) to the center medallion along the left side of the border satin strip and similarly right row (Block No. 6–No. 8) to the right side of the satin border.

8) Stitch the top (Block No. 1–No. 5) and bottom (Block No. 9–No. 13) rows in the same manner to the center medallion joined with the left and right rows of blocks.

Borders

9) Stitch the shorter inside borders to left and right sides of the blocks and the longer inside borders.to the top and bottom of the blocks.

`EMBROIDERY

10) Select RomHrstquilt1SmallCorner from the *Latte Quilt* CD then transfer this design to the machine/card to embroider this design on the right side of the satin centered on the straight on four of the 7in satin squares and on the diagonal on the remaining four 7in satin squares.

NOTE: *This has already been done on the template.*

11) Use the following color sequence:
   - Color No. 1 Fawn
   - Color No. 2 Oat

12) Press the embroidered blocks over a towel from the wrong side of the satin then square the blocks down to 5¾in. Fuse the matching batting squares to the back of the embroidered blocks.

PIECING THE OUTSIDE BORDERS

13) Using the eight 5¾in embroidered squares on the right side of the satin and the eight 5¾in x 36¾in satin strips on the wrong side of the satin

14) **Piece the outside borders in the following way:**

   —sides, two 36¾in satin strips (wrong side) joined together in the center with an embroidered (on the straight 'v' to the center of the quilt) satin square, one for either side of the quilt

   —top and bottom, two 36¾in satin strips (wrong side) joined as above with an embroidered (on the diagonal 'v' to the center of the quilt) satin square on either end for the top and bottom of the quilt.

15) Stitch the borders to the quilt in the following sequence; left side, right side, top then bottom of the quilt.

16) Trim all sides of the quilt making sure the quilt is square.

BACKING AND BINDING

TIP: *Clear a large surface to put the two layers of the quilt together— remember we are using the quilt-as-you-go technique so we now apply the backing to the quilt.*

16) You can either use the quilters safety pins in the traditional way to secure the backing to the quilt at intervals starting from the center of the quilt and pinning to the outside edge of the quilt, or the quilt basting spray—whichever you feel suits your needs best. Either way you need to make sure there are no puckers in the backing fabric and that the fabrics are flat and smooth.

APPLYING QUILT BACKING WITH BASTING SPRAY

For large areas such as the *Latte Quilt* have a large cleared surfaces, such as the floor of your garage or a tiled area, with windows and doors open. Cover the area either with paper or sheeting that can be washed, making sure it exceeds the size of the quilt by at least one foot on all sides.

Lay the quilt over the covered floor, with the batting side uppermost then center the backing over the batting. Roll the backing fabric back to one edge. Sparingly apply the basting spray to one foot of the batting adjacent to the rolled-up backing, let dry for around a minute then unroll the backing over the sprayed batting, pressing the fabric to the batting and making sure there are no puckers.

Continue in this way until the backing fabric is un-rolled and basted to the batting. Should you be quilting in the traditional way you can sandwich the batting between the quilt top and the backing in the same way.

Tip: *Should the backing fabric come away in any area, a hot steam iron will activate the basting spray and reapply the backing fabric.*

17) Apply the Jinny Beyer backing fabric to the back of the *Latte Quilt* then quilt in the following way using matching thread to the fabric area being quilted and bobbin thread to match the backing fabric:

—stitch-in-the-ditch in all the seams using the walking foot and the open-toe

—stipple-quilt the center of the quilt using the photo as a guide. On the border triangles with the appliquéd hearts stipple-quilt up to the muslin and around the hearts on the wrong side of the satin area only

—outline quilt using monofilament thread and the freehand quilting foot around the appliquéd hearts and any of the embroidered motifs in the blocks you choose —the more you do the better your quilt will look.

—stipple-quilt the quilt borders on the dull side of the satin only ommitting the embroidered satin squares.

18) Join the binding satin strips into a continuous length then fold in half lengthwise with the wrong side of the satin facing in and pressing from the right side.

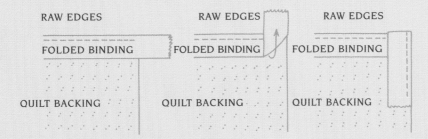

RAW EDGES   RAW EDGES   RAW EDGES

FOLDED BINDING   FOLDED BINDING   FOLDED BINDING

QUILT BACKING   QUILT BACKING   QUILT BACKING

19)   Pin then stitch to the outside of the quilt using a ¼in seam with the folded edge of the satin facing the center of the quilt and the raw fabric edges of the quilt and the binding aligned. Pleat each corner as you go around the quilt.

20)   Leave a 2in 'tail' of binding at the start of stitching, stopping the binding 2in before you complete attaching the binding to the quilt.

21)   Join the binding by opening it out flat pinning the right sides of the binding together and stitching from the wrong side at the desired length, trimming the seam to ¼in then pressing the seam flat. Fold the binding in half lengthwise again and press, then pin and stitch the rest of the way around the quilt as before to complete the binding.

22)   Press then pin the binding to the back of the quilt, matching the pleats at the corners to the front of the quilt then hand sew in place using a hand sewing needle and thread.

23)   Sign and date your quilt with pride. You may choose to do as we have using an embroidered frame to encase your name and the date.

97

Latte Inspirations
for the
Linen Cupboard

Stitches used on Blocks

Block 1, 5, 9 and 13
From CPS stitch No 603 width 9.0mm length 1.25mm
From the machine stitch No 416 width 7.0mm density 0.3mm
From CPS stitch No 740 width 9.0mm length 2.25mm
From the machine stitch No 102 default width and length
From the machine stitch No 110 default width and length

Blocks 2 and 10
From the CPS stitch No 732 width 3.0mm length 3.5mm
From the CPS stitch No 732 default width and length

From the machine stitch No 309 width and length 4.0mm
From the machine stitch No 702 width 3.0mm length 3.5mm

Blocks 3 and 11
From the CPS stitch No 431 width 5.0mm length 1.25mm
From the CPS stitch No 135 default width and length

Block 4 and 12
From the machine stitch No 708 width 6.0mm and length 2.5mm

Block 6 and 14
From the machine stitch No 407 width 4.0mm and length 0.25mm
From the machine stitch No 117 default width and length

Block 7 and 15
From the machine stitch No 117 default width and length

Block 8 and 16

From the machine stitch No 407 width 6.0mm and length 0.25mm

Center Embroidered Block

From the machine stitch No 2 width 2.0mm density 0.3mm
From the CPS stitch No 732 width 3.0mm length 1.25mm

From the CPS stitch No 732 default width and length

Center Medallion Appliqué

From the machine stitch No 2 width 2.0mm density 0.3mm
From the CPS stitch No 427 default width and length
From the CPS stitch No 732 default width and length